MW00535379

Avoiding the Fifth Point of Contact:

The Gray Zone: Achieving in an Imperfect System

Darren Hargrove

DORRANCE
PUBLISHING CO
EST. 1920
PITTSBURGH, PENNSYLVANIA 15238

Dorrance Publishing Co
585 Alpha Drive
Pittsburgh, PA 15238
Visit our website at *www.dorrancebookstore.com*

ISBN: 978-1-6470-2251-8
eISBN: 978-1-6470-2867-1

Our Deepest Fear

"Our deepest fear is not that we are inadequate. Our deepest fear is that we are powerful beyond measure. It is our light, not our darkness that most frightens us. We ask ourselves, Who am I to be brilliant, gorgeous, talented, fabulous? Actually, who are you NOT to be? You are a child of God. Your playing small does not serve the world. There is nothing enlightened about shrinking so that other people won't feel insecure around you. We are all meant to shine, as children do. We were born to make manifest the glory of God that is within us. It's not just in some of us; it's in everyone. And as we let our own light shine, we unconsciously give other people permission to do the same. As we are liberated from our own fear, our presence automatically liberates others."

Marianne Williamson

Contents

Purpose

Friends of mine ask me, why write a book? I thought about it for a minute and told them that if I can help one person with the words I write, then that would satisfy my reason for writing this book.

Sometimes being a leader is tough and not for the weak-minded. So why do people want to lead or be in leadership positions? Most people think they can make a difference. As a leader, you have to realize that things will get tougher, not easier. Senior leaders must express to our young leaders that to accomplish the mission and taking of their subordinates in a less than perfect system without the appropriate resources or time to get it done will be the way things are a majority of the time. That means that you have to get off your knees and stop praying for "quality" and develop the "qualified."

This book is about your character and how to avoid situations that put your character into question. Simply put, gracefully eat shit instead of kissing ass to be successful and not have your character to ever be in question. That is the difference between the haves and have-nots. Even doing the right things does not always equate to the success you want or deserve. We have to inspire future leaders of not thinking promotions as a measure of success; this is a trap because it is not guaranteed. Even the Monday-through-Friday, nine-to-five leader can get promoted. Being successful is different from being great! Things will not always come when you want them. You may have to go through many other things to get to where you want to be in life.

I spent a little over thirty years in uniform, and I saw a lot people achieve their goals, while on the other hand, many more that didn't. The main reason between the two is simple: mindset. I can relate this to an article I read called "The Birdcage Theory."

According to Marilyn Frye, the Birdcage Theory explains the wires on a birdcage. From this microscopic perspective you would not understand how a bird could ever be contained by such a futile device. Inspecting the wire from all angles, up and down, was in this way. Furthermore, you could even inspect multiple wire devices has no bearing on a bird's mobility. After all, there is nothing about any one of these singular wires that would compromise the bird's mobility, except in the most accidental way. It is only when you take a step back and view the cage from a macroscopic perspective that you see the wires as a network of systematically related barriers, working together to contain the bird. What most people don't realize is that there is a door on the birdcage. You just have to find the door on the birdcage. The worst person you will have to deal with is the one that has given up hope finding the door on the birdcage.

No matter what you do in your life, you will always have obstacles that will limit or restrict you from achieving your goals. What matters is how you maneuver around and through those barriers in your life. You will always have something that will hamper you from achieving your goals. It can be people, current job, finances, limited resources, or a combination of different things. The key is how you handle yourself during the tough times.

I never let someone or something else control my life or what I wanted to do with my life. I didn't always get the job or assignment I wanted, but I made sure that I maximized the opportunity I had in front of me. That is what this book is about. If you don't get the job you want, be the best you can in the job you get. If you don't have the resources you need to accomplish your job, make the best use of the resources you have in that job. If you didn't get the promotion you expected, capitalize on your abilities in your current position.

The bottom line is to take advantage of what you have while in the meantime still striving to achieve your goals. Don't let your individual birdcage make you unable to find the door.

What are Gray Zone Leaders?

Have you ever heard the expression, "I will respect SFC Smith's rank/position, but I don't respect SFC Smith as a person"? Do you know what it really means? During the senior enlisted promotion boards, there are three categories: Best Qualified, the Gray Zone, and NCOs considered for the Qualitative Management Program (QMP). "Gray Zone Leaders" are the ones that are in the middle of the pack. The "Gray Zone Leaders" are the ones that their records have to be voted on again to see if they are getting promoted. SFC Smith could be one of those Gray Zone Leaders.

As leaders, we wear our LBE every day. I am not talking about Load Bearing Equipment but Leading By Example. We cannot pick and choose which regulations we want to follow or enforce. Gray Zone Leaders only enforce the one they agree with or the ones in line with their way of thinking. You cannot pick and choose which regulations or rules you want to follow.

We have to realize that the higher we go in rank, the higher the number of people looking to leaders for guidance. If leaders are not giving maximum effort, then our subordinate leaders will think that is how things are supposed to be done. Every time a leader does not correct a substandard situation, no matter what it is, then a new standard has been set.

We are getting to the point where the Army is looking to retain the "Best Qualified." If you are in that "Gray Zone" and your record has to be voted on again, then you may not make the cut. This could have significant career consequences when it comes time to downsize the force. Every leader wakes up in the morning knowing who they are and what they are willing to become. The hard part is being honest with yourself.

My mentor once told me a story about four kinds of leaders, one of which is the unwilling but able Soldier. An able but unwilling leader possesses the full capacity to excel but for various reasons, succumbs to complacency, has a lack of personal courage, or an overall lack of desire to persevere. Another way to say it is this way: the worst types of Soldier are the ones who don't do what they are supposed to do or the ones who **ONLY** do what they are supposed to do. This is a Gray Zone Leader. What kind of leader are you and how do you stay out of the Gray Zone?

How Do You Know if You are a Gray Zone Leader?

When we were stationed in Germany, I was watching AFN, and for those who have lived overseas, you know all of the military history and good to know information AFN shows. Well, I heard one story that really caught my attention, and I think about it all the time. The story is about after a tidal wave washed a bunch of starfish to the shore, along came a little boy who started to throw the starfish back into the water one by one. Then came this gentleman and asked the boy did he think that he could make a difference to all of the starfish?

The little boy threw another starfish into the water and politely said, "I made a difference to that one!" That is why I want you to find your starfish and make a difference for that one. The best place to find your starfish is where I call the gray zone and find what I like to call the Gray Zone Soldier. I know you are asking "what are the gray zone and a Gray Zone Soldier?"

You have heard of the term "Gray Zone" from the senior NCO promotion boards. That is when your record goes into the "Gray Zone" to be voted on again to see if you **JUST** did enough to get promoted.

Well, the "Gray Zone Soldiers" are the ones that are in the middle of the pack. The Gray Zone Soldier is the one that goes to the physical fitness test only trying to pass instead of scoring a 300 plus each and every time. These types of Soldiers are the ones that go to the different military schools only to achieve course standards rather than to exceed the course standards.

These types of Soldiers are always borderline within the standards of AR 600-9 and fail to maintain their weight year-round. These types of Soldiers only conduct negative event-oriented counseling or perform no counseling at all. They fail to mentor and do only what is necessary to "check the block."

They are the ones that can tell you about every club in that area and surrounding areas but cannot tell you which way to the education center or library.

They are also the ones that have been in the unit the longest and can tell you everything wrong with the unit but do not contribute to making the unit better. They pick and choose which regulations they want to follow or enforce because that is the one they agree with or is in line with their way of thinking. Now I know what you are thinking, "Yeah, I know that type of Soldier!" This type of Soldier possesses the full capacity to excel but for various reasons, succumbs to complacency, has a lack of personal courage, or an overall lack of desire to persevere.

This is a Gray Zone Leader. Most of the time, this type of leader cannot see them in this type of light. When you tell someone they are this way, either they do not or cannot believe it; something I heard before always comes to my mind.

I grew up about ten miles away from my grandmother. My grandmother was one of those grandmothers who had an answer for everything and put in a way you could understand it in the simplest form. She and I had a really close relationship, and I learned a lot from her.

One day I was at her house and can remember we were talking about a situation I was in and telling her how everyone was labeling me as having a bad attitude. She looked directly at me and just said, "Baby everybody can't be wrong." The more I thought about it, the more I realized that I did have a bad attitude. Those words have stuck with me ever since that summer day.

Everybody can't be wrong. There might be certain cases where everyone might judge a person one way and that person turns out to be totally different from what everybody thought. Those occasions are rare. Other than those rare occasions, people turn out how everyone sees that person. It is not to say that you are that person, but it is what people see and how you treat them that will determine how you are to the rest of the world, good or bad.

Whatever image you portray, then that is what people think. For example, if you dress a certain way or style that is how you want people to see you, and that is how people will judge you before they will have a chance to get to know you on a different level. The same thing will happen with the words that come out of your mouth. If you talk in an uneducated way, then that is the way you will be judged. People will form their opinion of you first based on what they see and then what they hear. People will see the outer you before getting to know that inter you. So, whatever you present to people is what will be your calling card.

Now, the more time you are with those some people then a different image or the real you might emerge from their first impression of you. One of the best ways to do this is when you take new leadership jobs. If everybody thinks that you are a pushover, then that is how you will be taken. It is the same as if everybody thinks you are unfair, hard, or any other adjective that describes a person.

See, there has to be a reason why people think you are the way you are because you had to be that way to everyone you meet. If you want people to know the real you, then you need to present the real you. You cannot cuss like a rapper, but you want people to think that you are a choir boy. The two just don't mix. You cannot treat everyone you meet unfairly but think that you are a fair person; then who is right and who is wrong?

So, when I run into a Gray Zone Leader, they tell me that they are not like that, I would simply say "Well, like Granny Hargrove would say 'everyone can't be wrong.'"

The Gray Zone Leader is the worst type of leader because they are the ones that **only** do what they are supposed to do or **do not** do what they are supposed to do. Neither one of those traits is good, nor what you look for in a leader along with what you want to deal with on a daily basis.

Doing what they are supposed to do, mean that they come to work right on time, leave for lunch on time, and go home right on time every day. They push things off until tomorrow and never do a follow-up on the things they set aside for later. They counsel their subordinates only when they have too and never do it for the benefit of the subordinate.

This type of person will never go above and beyond what is required of them just to make it through the day. They are not looking for new ideas to improve their area. Everything else in their life is always more important than their job. They always have a problem doing anything outside of their duty description. They are also the ones that you have a tough time trying to write their evaluation because they don't do anything great but not enough to get them in trouble. They are just successful, nothing more nothing less, the middle of the road.

The ones that don't do what they are supposed to do. They are the ones that are always late with their reports and constantly contain errors. They are the ones that are always unorganized. They never counsel their subordinates and give everyone the same rating to keep them from complaining.

Their subordinates are always unhappy with them. They are the ones their subordinates are happier when they are not at work. They are the ones that can never be found when there is something going on in their area. They are the ones that never know what are the newest policies or updates because they don't take the time to find out. They are the ones that make more excuses to why something is not done instead of just getting it done. They are the ones that always think that everybody is out to get them and always want to file a complaint against the chain of command instead of just doing their jobs. They are the ones that will not hold anyone to the standard when it comes to their job.

Most of the time, the supervisor of the Gray Zone Leaders is one themselves or did not take the time to train the Gray Zone Leaders suitably to do better. This type of person showed those traits when they were the worker bees. We tend to recommend subpar people for the next higher job based on time in their present job or they are doing so-so in their job just because someone has to move up, so they are the lesser of the two evils. These shouldn't be the reasons to promote or recommend someone for promotion.

Leadership traits should be used, like if someone can actually lead other people, to recommend someone for promotion. Telling someone that they are not ready for the next step will not hurt that person; it will help them by telling them the areas they lack in to improve their leadership skills.

Everyone was not meant to be a leader. When we try to put everyone in leadership positions, then you tend to end up with the Gray Zone Leaders. Some people are satisfied with being a worker bee, while other strives to be leaders. As a leader, you need to identify the difference between the two and choose the best one to put in the leadership position.

How Do You Stay Out of the Gray Zone?

If you don't have direction, then how do you know which way you are going? *(Before you are ready to lead someone, you have to know where you want to be in life. If you're still at a standstill in your life, then there is no way you are able to help someone else to move forward in theirs.)*

It's not how you start but how you finish. *(You have the power to change your situation. If you start out one way, doesn't mean you have to stay that way. Understand your current situation, know where you want to be, realize what it takes to get there, and just go and do it!)*

You will not reach your goals more by doubt than failure. *(Don't let negative thoughts, people, or situations control you and keep you from your goals. Because someone else you know failed, doesn't mean you will.)*

You are more than one-dimensional, so you have to stop thinking that way. *(You have to see the second, third, and fourth order of your decision. A one-dimensional thinker is a person that sees things right in front of them. If you make a decision based on how you feel or think today and never worrying about how that decision will impact your life later, then you are a one-dimensional thinker. Everyone thinks about their future.)*

Be the example; people will follow you more by the example you set than the words you speak. *(People should see you as a leader and not just hear you speak about one. The way you carry yourself should speak volumes on what type of leader you are, and you will never have to convince someone otherwise.)*

You have to get into a position in order to change the game. (Get in the game and learn the game.) *(If you are not happy with the way things are run in your job, then get in the position of power [power = responsibilities, resources, and information] to make the changes. It is easy to tell others what they should be doing when you don't have a stake in the outcome. But when you are the one that is taking the risk by the decisions that are made, then you will be more aware of your actions, words, and decisions you make.)*

You have to understand the strategic in order to be able to explain the operational and tactical. *(If you don't know what the leaders above you are doing or thinking, then you will never be able to translate it to your peers and subordinates. You have to be able to see and understand the world in order to explain how it works.)*

Never take advice from someone you wouldn't trade places with. *(If I've already surpassed you, what can you really tell me?)*

Don't be ineffective or incompetent because neither one is good. *(Either people have stopped listening to you, or they realized you don't know what you are doing; once you get to that point, then things will only get better once you leave.)*

Don't lose your mind when things get dark because you will need your mind when those things become light again. *(Because things didn't go right for you at that particular time doesn't mean you have to throw everything away; don't make a rash decision at the age of twenty-five that can affect you at the age of forty-five)*

Those who allow their inner light to shine then they have no need for the spotlight. *(When you are genuinely doing it for others, then there is no need for you to look for their admiration; they will give it to you automatically.)*

I heard a story once, about a keyboard and a piano. Life is like playing a keyboard versus a piano. It all depends who is sitting at the bench playing the keys. If someone is sitting at the piano and the only thing they can play is *Mary had a Little Lamb*, then people begin to believe that is all the piano has to offer. On the other hand, if you have someone on the keyboard playing everything from jazz to gospel, then one might believe the keyboard is better and has a lot more to offer. But if we switch the one playing the keyboard with the one playing the piano, then people with realize that the only thing that matters is the one who is playing the keys. So, who is playing the keys in your life?

The Total Soldier Concept

I remember one day when I was in the Sergeants Major Academy with my small group and the discussion navigated to the total Soldier concept. One of my battle buddies made the comment about how his old Division Command Sergeant Major (CSM) was great at physical training, and that was his main focal point. He went on to say how if the leadership did not score a certain score (290 out of 300, I think) on their physical fitness test, that they would get only a success in leadership on their Noncommissioned Officer Evaluation Report (NCOER).

Me being me, I was like, really? So, I asked him did he have the same focus on Soldiers going to school, and if they did not achieve at least a 90 percent GPA, were they going to get the same in leadership, a success, on their NCOERs? Better yet, if they did not complete a certain amount of hours while taking college courses or correspondence courses, would they get the same rating? Of course the answer was no!

I do not have anything against the CSM trying to push the leadership to do well in PT. The division was a rapid deployable division, and physical fitness is a must. Not just in that division but in the Army as a whole. My problem was the CSM's center of attention was on one aspect of the total Soldier concept. It is great that a Soldier can run a 12:30 on the two miles and score 300 (the maximum) on the physical fitness test, but if that same Soldier is not able to perform his or her job, what good is that Soldier to the unit or the Army?

The total Soldier concept makes the Soldiers better and more competitive. You want Soldiers that can perform well in all areas of his or her job and not just excel in one area and perform subpar in all of the rest. Your job as a leader is to identify where the future leaders are weak and help them improve in those areas.

One way to do this is to have the Soldiers perform an annual self-assessment. If the Soldier is true with themself and perform the self-assessment, then they can determine along with their supervisors the areas that they are weak in and ways to improve those areas. If you are not true to yourself, then there is no way you can be truthful to others. Now, a lot of people are first to find fault in others but never in themselves. The ones who do that will never grow and develop. We all know those types of people. They are the ones that always say, "I did this or I did that," or "when I was this or when I was that." They were the greatest thing that unit ever saw, but the bad thing about that is no one that knew that person could validate those claims.

Usually, it is the other way around. That person did not do anything in the unit but complain along with causing problems after problems. The ones that grow and evolve are the ones that let their actions speak for them and let the others around them be their mouthpiece. If you are true to the ones around you, then they will tell your story of how great you are!

Another way is to put those Soldiers in charge of a task. One of the best ways to see how someone performs in a stressful situation is to put them in charge of the situation. Give them a task, some direction and guidance, and check on them later. This is a way to separate your top performers from the ones that are just good performers from the ones who just cannot perform at all.

If you are looking for someone to take your place when you leave, you should prepare someone who has the ability to perform in all aspects of the job and not just one or two performance areas. It is your job to find the complete Soldiers in the formations and continue to challenge them by improving their abilities to lead in the future.

Premier Protégè

L ife is about Making Choices *(Goals without a plan are just wishes and dreams)*
Everyone wants to be successful in life. Regardless of what you do, we all have that internal drive to be the best at your chosen profession. The difference is that some people's drive is stronger than others. We have all been in class when we were younger, and the teacher asked, "What do you want to be when you grow up?"

Everyone would say policeman, firefighter, teacher, or some type of professional athlete to name a few. While at that age, you never thought about what it took to make those dreams become reality, better yet what it took to get to the pinnacle of that career. A lot of times, we see the product of someone's career but never stop to wonder how they got to that point.

There are many pathways to professional advancement, and one is neither easier nor more difficult than the next, but what it really depends on is you. Are you willing to do what it takes to achieve those senior level positions or be considered the best at what you do? Many people have no desire to be in those top positions, which are fine, but for those who want to achieve those top echelons in their line of business, you have to find out what it takes to get there.

The initial step is to find out what you like to do. I am pretty sure for most of us the dream we had in elementary school is different from the occupation you have now. If you do something you like, nine times out of ten you will take ownership of that job to become exceptional. After you have decided on your preferred field, next is where you want to see yourself in five, ten, fifteen, and twenty years from now. If you cannot see yourself at the peak of your chosen profession, then you cannot get there.

You have to set goals for yourself, and one way to do this is starting an Individual Development Plan (IDP) and meeting those career goals you have set for yourself. With goal setting, the goals have to be realistic. Not many, and I mean a very few, can go from the mailroom to the CEO of the company in five years unless they have the same last name of the person who owns the company. That brings me to my next point, which is to work hard, learn all you can about your job by becoming the subject matter expert or "go-to" person, and having patience. There are probably less than two percent of all professionals that are able to make it to the top, be successful, and be labeled as "the youngest to achieve this or that." The other 98 percent have to put in the hours, be proficient when conducting their business and wait their turn. Once you get there, you have to know what you are doing to stay there or even go further up that ladder of success. The next thing is to find a mentor. Before you chose that mentor, there are two things that you need to consider, which are "never receive counsel from unproductive people and never discuss your problems with someone incapable of contributing to the solution, because those who never succeed themselves are always first to tell you how." (Powell, n.d.)

"Your mentor should be the person that you have placed in a high position in your life, to guide your path, direction, and future." (Lewis, 2011). The sad part is that many of us have placed the wrong person in this position. The way to know if you have placed the wrong person is to measure your progress. "Are you at a standstill? Have you been walking in the same steps for the past few years? Has anything significant changed in your life because of you choosing this person as your mentor? Well, if your answer is no, then you have placed the wrong person in front of you, and you are marking the wrong steps." (Unknown, n.d.)

There is only one person who is capable of setting limits to your growth: it is you. "Your life does not change when your boss changes, when your friends change, when your parents change, when your husband or wife changes, when your company changes, when your church changes, when your location changes, when your money changes, when your status changes. Your life changes when you change, when you go beyond your limiting beliefs. Examine yourself, watch yourself. Don't be afraid of difficulties, impossibilities and losses. Be a winner; build yourself and your reality. It's the way you face life that makes the difference!" (Oluyi, 2011) Your attitude affects your aptitude, which in turn affects your altitude.

You cannot measure your success off someone else's achievements nor can you judge your success off someone else's goals. You have to set goals for yourself and meet them. If you achieve the goals you have set for yourself, enjoy your success. You cannot live up to goals that someone else has set for you because it might not be what you want for yourself. Do not let someone tell you that you are not successful because you did not reach benchmarks set by others. Not everyone wants the same dreams out of life. You cannot live peacefully by trying to live up to someone else's expectations of you. You are only going to be the best at something if it is what you want for yourself and something you want to do.

Your car, job, house, or nothing else you have are not the things that make you successful but your happiness that you set goals for yourself, and you have reached those goals. A simple but steady life for some people is all they need while others need the limelight. Remember that old saying "keeping up with the Joneses;" well the Joneses might be broke and/or unhappy. I cannot remember how many times I have seen television shows like, *Behind the Music, E! True Hollywood Story, Where are They Now*, or some similar show and all the struggles those rich, and so-called successful people encounter in their everyday life. "With some people you spend an evening, with others you invest it. Be careful where you stop to inquire for directions along the road of life. Wise is the person who fortifies his life with the right friendships." (Powell, n.d.)

I did not pick your job, so why are you mad at me?

When I was a sergeant in Korea, I was on one of the smaller camps there. After a while, you will get to know everybody or at least where they worked. I would always see this specialist/E-4 (SPC) working in the dining facility that seemed to be upset with the world. He never changed his attitude or the disdainful look he had on his face every time I went into the Dining Facility (DFAC). One day, I saw the SPC at the Post Exchange (PX) and so I just had to ask him why was he so upset all the time. He told me that he hated his job, and it was not what he expected when he joined.

So, I begin to ask him what was he doing to change his situation, and he said nothing. I ask him about what he wanted to do in life, which he said he didn't know. I asked him about his education level, which he told me that he was a high school graduate. He started telling me about how his work kept him from going to college, and the story went on and on why he couldn't do this and why he couldn't do that. I gave him all types of scenarios that he could follow to get him into something that he liked, and I heard more excuses, so it wasn't worth my time to continue. He started to get upset with me because I was asking him a lot of questions, and he could see that I wasn't buying his excuses because every time he gave me one, I would give him a counter to his excuses.

Thus, after all that, I just asked him, "Then why are you mad at me? I didn't pick your job." He gave me this stare, and I told him the person he should be mad at was himself because he was the one that decided not to do anything to change his situation. No one but you can change your situation. If you are in a job that you do not like, why are you staying there? You and you only know what you want to do to be happy in your life. If you are not doing anything to change it, then that means you are satisfied with your current situation. Most of the time change starts with an elevation in your educational level.

Ever since I can remember, people have been stating that if you want to live the American dream then education needs to be a part of it. Why are you in a dead-end job? Why are you in a job with no room for growth or progression? There are a few, and I mean very few, jobs in the world today that you can have growth within that job without some type of education for that job. During the 2012 presidential elections, I remember one of the candidates referred to the president as a "snob" for wanting everyone to go to college. The candidate said, "What if the person wanted to be a mechanic?" The first thought that came to my mind was, mechanics go to school because when I am getting repairs done on my car, I would see their Automotive Service Excellence (ASE) certificates hanging on the walls. That means that they are not just the old "shade tree" mechanics that I grew up around but properly taught certified mechanics. So, how can furthering your career through education be a bad thing?

You have to ask yourself a question, and that is "are you an asset or liability to your company?" Are you not just keeping up but moving ahead of the current trends and technology? Will being educated in your field alone make you an asset to your company? There are different mindsets people have with other people who have earned a degree. The bottom line is that you have the capacity to learn, and you put the time and effort in to get it. That holds a lot of weight with people. If you have a degree, people without one will treat you differently when they first meet you.

I know you have heard of a sports star that thought his or her talent alone would get them to the top, but it is not like that. Talent will get you in the door, but hard work, knowing what you are doing, dedication, and continuous progression will keep you there and help you to move higher.

Does the thought of success frighten you?

"Keeping it real!" I have heard this phrase over and over during the last few years. It means do not forget where you came from and don't be a fake person. Which is great, but if that same phrase is keeping you from succeeding in life because you are afraid of what people whom you know will think, is that really keeping it real? When you start holding your potential back, to be successful, just because of what your so-called friends might think, then who will be hurt in the long run?

As a parent, you should want your kids to do better than you. You make sacrifices so they can have better opportunities to do better for themselves. A lot of times, we let outside sources persuade us, especially when we are young, to do things other than succeed or at least do what is right to succeed.

We like to hide the fact that we are smart or want to do something better than the situation you are in now, and we allow people to make us feel bad by wanting to do something else with your life other than staying in your same hometown. The only thing you have to look forward to is waiting for the ones who left to come home for the different holidays so you can be with them and they will tell you how life is outside your comfort zone.

Why do people like to celebrate the fact that someone gets out of prison for a crime they committed over the fact of someone graduating from college. I have seen it where someone traveled over a hundred miles, one way, to go to their nephew's BBQ for getting out of jail but would not travel sixty miles, round trip, to see their two nieces' graduate (one with honors) from college. Now when that same uncle has money problems because he has them all the time, which one of his relatives is he going to go to for help?

I have also heard the phrase "Oh you think that you are better than me" because I decided to shoot for the moon. Well, I am here to tell you that it is not the person who has done something with their life thought process. It is the one who has nothing to do all day way of thinking. The ones who are trying to achieve more do not have time to think whom they are better than. The other ones try to make you feel bad about achieving more. Those are the people you need to keep out of your life. They are the ones that make you want to be like them by allowing them to choke your dreams.

When I was younger, my friend's brother was a very good football player in high school. His senior year, he received a lot of scholarship offers from major Division I colleges and universities. A few of us really looked up to him mostly because we were football players and we wanted the same kind of success he had in high school, like being able to receive scholarship offers from different colleges and universities. He was close to our age, and like I said earlier, his brother was one of my friends, so I knew him pretty well.

He ended up going to a junior college, transferred to a Division I-AA school where he did not play football, and then his life went downhill from there. I have not seen him in years, but he wasn't doing a lot with his life. The last time I saw him, I was in my hometown, and another friend (who is now an assistant basketball coach, for a Division I program) of mine I grew up with was coming out of a store when we saw him. The first thing he said to us was we were not going to do anything with our lives just like he didn't. We were shocked by what he said.

My friend told him that is not going to happen, and those words gave us motivation that we needed to succeed in our chosen field. I would think he would tell us not to follow in his footsteps because we looked up to him when we were younger, but he was so disappointed in the way his life turned out, he wanted everyone to end up the same way he did, not living up to your true potential.

That is not keeping it real to me. Keeping it real is realizing your true potential in life and not letting those doubters stopping you from making it happen. Despite what you do in life, you will have people who will doubt you and not want you to do well. Do not be afraid of those with doubt in their minds about what lies ahead for you in your life. How would they know what lies ahead for you if you do what it takes to keep it real for yourself? Only you can stop your success!

If someone wants you to do bad or try to persuade you to do something bad, are they really looking out for your best interest?
I have seen this situation a lot in my life. Do you put your trust and faith in someone who continually wants you to do bad or the wrong thing? Why? If they are not looking out for your best interests, then what are they looking out for? The majority of the time, that same individual, did not do anything with his or her life when they had the opportunity and wanted you to do the same.

You can go with misery loves company or whatever cliché you want to go with because they all hold true when we are talking about someone choking your dreams. How many times have you been in or seen a situation where someone knew better but did it anyway, continued to let a so-called friend drink, knowing they have had enough, even worse letting their friend drink and drive? How about someone trying to do homework but wants you to go to the club? This is a classic example of a Gray Zone Leader. These people always want you to do the wrong thing.

You have to figure those people out and do it in a hurry. You have to ask yourself two questions; if they have achieved their goals, then why do they not want you to achieve yours or if they have not achieved their goals, then why do they not want you to achieve yours? Either way, this is still a person you do not want or need in your life. If you do not ask yourself why is this person, who's supposed to be helping you end up hurting you in the long run?

At a certain point in your life, you have to realize that it is not important to fit in with certain people or groups anymore. Because the less you associate with some people, the more your life will improve. Any time you endure mediocrity in others, it increases your mediocrity. An imperative characteristic in successful people is their impatience with negative thinking and negative acting people. As you grow, your acquaintances will change.

See, if this person can tell you where every dance club, strip joint, and party spot is in the city but cannot tell you how to find the education center or how to start your savings plan, then you might want to be wary of that person unless that is what you want out of life. On the other hand, this person also may be the one that is afraid that you might pass them up and lead you down a road where you might not want to go.

These types of people are the worst because they have preplanned this in their mind that they are going to do you wrong in some way or another. They have spent a majority of their time messing around, and now they might have decided to get their life in order but do not want you to do the same. They will tell you all the wrong things or give you the half-truths. "Some of your friends will not want you to go on with your life. They want you to stay where they are because friends that don't help you climb, want you to crawl. Your friends will stretch your vision or choke your dream. Those that don't increase you will eventually decrease you." (Powell, n.d.)

Intermediate Scholar

Never lose your power base

You can lose your power base two ways: by not supporting your chain of command or by putting yourself in a situation where your duty position (job) may come into question. You will not always agree with the decisions that are made by your leadership. When you are in a leadership position, it is not your job to always to agree but to execute the mission as it is given.

Ever since I was a 1SG and had my initial counseling with my commander, I would tell them that if we agree on something, then you will get 100 percent out of me. If we don't agree, then you will get 110 percent out of me because that is what it will take for me to execute that particular mission. I always wanted my commander to know that they had my support either way and even more so when we disagreed.

No matter what type of relationship you are involved in, you will not always agree with that person 100 percent of the time, but if you care about the relationship and want it to move forward, you have to show support especially in times of adversity. You can't pick and choose when you want to be a leader but to be a leader 24/7/365.

I see that a lot when people are in a disagreement; it shows, and it goes throughout the organization. If you truly care about the organization, you will show your support. If you don't like how things are going in the organization, then get in a position to make changes.

I heard one CSM say that when he was a private, he stated that when he gets in the squad leader position that he won't make those same bad decisions his squad leader did that made things bad in his squad. He said that for every rank he held until he made CSM, then he realized that he did not have anyone else to point the finger at but himself. The point of the story is simple: if you are not part of the solution, then you are part of the problem. You cannot lead them if you are one of them.

A leader has to know when being one of the boys is no longer part of your DNA makeup. You are put in charge of them to lead them. Continuing being part of the in-crowd is not an option. You can lose your power base by putting yourself in awkward situations. People can see you not supporting the command, so why should they support you.

If you are not leading by example—like if you require your employees to be on time, but you come late to work every day. You cannot be out in the clubs every weekend doing things that are seen to be in a distasteful manner with your employees and expect them to follow your orders the following week at work. You cannot show favoritism towards employees you supervise, especially the ones that are assumed friends. This list could go on and on, but the bottom line is, once you lose your power base, it is almost impossible to get it back.

It is one of the most important things you have but can lose as a leader if your employees presume any unfair practices at the workplace. As long as everyone knows who is in charge, then you might have an easier time trying to get people to follow your lead. If they have to question your sincerity as a leader, then your days will be long and hard.

If you are the smartest person
in your group, then you need to find a new group

If you are the smartest person in your group, then you need to find you a new group. Iron sharpens iron; wood cannot sharpen iron. If you run with wolves, you will learn how to howl. If you associate with eagles, you will learn how to soar to great heights. Surround yourself with people who are trying to go in the same direction and reach the same goals you are because it does two things for you. One, you will keep that competitive fire in your stomach to keep moving forward, and two, you can see someone else that is going through the same things you are going through, so you know it can be done.

We always talk about being proactive versus reactive. Most of the time, your life will fit into one of those categories. Many of life's challenges you face will depend on whether you are proactive versus reactive. A proactive person is one who usually plans for things ahead of time. A reactive person is one who always has to react to a situation. Well, this holds true for the statement "If you are the smartest person in your group, then you need to find a new group." (Powell, n.d.)

This means making new connections with the people who are in a position that you are striving to reach or at least headed in the same direction you are going. A lot of times this means leaving some old associates behind. The proactive person can see themselves five, ten, fifteen years down the road and make plans on how to get to where they want to be. One big way is to surround themselves with positive people and people who are going somewhere. A proactive person is not intimidated by another person's success but rather sees what it took for that person to get to where they are and is willing to take some of the same routes to get there. The way to do that is to be where they are and know what they know.

A reactive person, on the other hand, always makes excuses about their future and they let the cards fall where they may. They like hanging around people who do not bring anything to the table. They tend to walk away from people whom they believe are successful in their line of work because they might feel intimidated or uncomfortable because they have doubt in their own abilities. Reactive people always like to stay in their own comfort zone and are not willing to stretch their boundaries. They enjoy their group of people because they are "the big man" on campus, so to speak. In the military, as well as life, the ones who are really successful are the ones that are not afraid of the challenges of life.

I was in a small Military Occupation Specialty (MOS) in the military. By the time you reach the senior levels, you know about 90 percent of the people in those senior positions and have heard of the other 10 percent. That makes it easy for most individuals because they know a lot of their coworkers and they feel comfortable around the people they work for and work with over the years. I consider them the reactive people or the ones that want to stay being the smartest person in their group. If you stay with the same circle of friends, you will just be recycling the same ideas over and over, so that means you will eventually end up at a standstill, which means no improvement in your profession. If you stay being a reactive person, then you may end up becoming irrelevant.

On the other hand, you have a select few that don't have a problem working outside of their career field, making new contacts, and learning new jobs. These are the proactive people. The proactive people, nine times out ten, will be better overall in just about every aspect of leadership more than the reactive people. The proactive person is always bringing something new to the table. They are the forward thinkers. They are the ones that are trying to take their unit to the next level by distain looking for new ways to improve the process.

Don't get me wrong; I am not saying that it is bad to have a group of friends that you like to hang around with just for a good time. We all have them, close friends of the family or someone you like to go to a ballgame with and just relax. But if that same group has been in the same situation for the last ten or fifteen years like barely getting by, not getting promoted, or just not doing anything, then you should have the other group of friends that you're hanging with to improve your life, then you put yourself in those situations where you can get the job done.

Are we making exceptions the normal way of business (slow cooked)?
I heard once that great NCOs have to be slow cooked. What does this mean? I am a Southern boy from Mississippi. Everyone I knew had a crock-pot or slow cooker. My mother would get up early in the morning or the night before to prepare her dinner for that Sunday. She would season, then marinade the meat, and after all of that was done, then she would place the meat in the slow cooker to let it cook all day. The longer it would cook, the better it smelled, and it was tender, and the taste could not be matched.

If you take that same meat and put it in the oven at about 450 degrees, the meat will be done on the outside but raw on the inside. You ask, why would you cook the meat at 450 degrees? Glad you asked, you did not prepare and plan your dinner, just got rushed, so you thought if you increase the temperature of the meat, then it will have the same effect because all you want is a finished product.

Well, we should take the same concept with our NCOs and Soldiers. They need to be slow cooked. The great NCOs are the ones that have the time to be trained and develop. The last few promotions boards, I have heard of a lot of NCOs bitter about not making the next rank, nothing new, right? After sitting down and talking to them, their chief complaint was about, for example, a Staff Sergeant/E-6 (SSG) not making Sergeant First Class/E-7 (SFC) in seven or eight years. When did this become the customary way of doing things and not the exception—SSG thinking that it is normal to make SFC in seven years? Well I am here to say that SFC in seven years *is* the exception. Only a select few SSG are ready to go to the Senior NCO ranks in less than ten years.

One thing that will always be the model and that is something you cannot teach: experience. About less than 10 percent of the NCOs get the experience they need to be a great or even good NCO in about ten years. One thing about being a leader is that you are always learning, but at the senior level your learning curve should be smaller than someone more junior to you, because of your experiences and simply put, your time in the Army. This does not apply to everyone because you may have someone who is junior but with more experience than someone who is senior. This is the exception that I was talking about. Being a great NCO is a marathon and not a sprint. More than anything it takes time. So, understand that great leadership is a slow process and something that should not be rushed if you want it to turn out right.

Tough challenge here. Learn to be more demure. "De mure." Adj. (Merriam-Webster, 1828)

1. Modest and reserved in manner or behavior.

2. Affectedly shy, modest, or reserved.

Speak quietly and carry a big brain. Get beyond being an NCO. Speak with authority when you speak, and speak loudly if you have to, but do most of your work quietly and steadily. But be an NCO. One of my great mentors said often that, "…if SGTs used all the authority given by law and regulation, they would scare all of us…."

Never receive counsel from unproductive people

You do not have to be in a rush to make the next rank; give yourself an opportunity to learn and grow. If you are doing what you are supposed to do and that is taking care of your Soldiers, then you will make the next rank. So many times you hear NCOs bragging about making a certain rank in a faster time frame than the average, but you never hear that same NCO bragging about how well they took care of their Soldiers. You let your Soldiers do the bragging for you with their actions and how well they execute their assignments.

Because you know how to cook, does not qualify you to give advice to a chef. This means because someone outranks you or is older does not mean that person can give you advice. I was on leave, and this person was older than

I was also spent some time in the military, so with those two things in his back pocket he thought that qualified him to give me advice. Not that I cannot receive advice, but he was not in the position to give me advice. First of all, the highest rank he said he achieved was E-6 in a different service and I was an E-8 at the time, and secondly he was trying to tell me how to buy a house, and he did not own the one he was in and as a matter of fact had never brought one in his life.

I am no better than anyone else. I just set my goals, stayed focus, and accomplished the goals I set for myself. It is amazing to me how someone who is doing no better than you ALWAYS wants to give you advice. Well, my advice to that person is to make sure you are doing better than the person you are trying to give advice to.

You cannot be one of those I would have, I should have, or I could have people and have someone listen to you about what they would have, should have, or could have done with their life or career. Success is about achieving your goals and not anyone else's, but if your goal was to make mailroom supervisor and the person you are trying to give advice to made CEO, it is hard to give that person advice on a lot of things.

A lot of people think because they are older, they can give you advice but have not experienced half the things you have but want to tell you how something is done. That is not always the case. If you have never bought a house, then how you can tell me how to, no matter what your age.

It is true that people who are senior to you in age can give you a lot of advice pertaining to life experiences, but it might be a little different for personnel in the military because of all of the different places we have lived and people we have met. It is hard for me to listen to someone who has lived in the same city or town all of their life trying to tell me about how to function in the world.

I might be younger in age, but it has to equal out if I have lived in and visited several countries around the world to include many of the states in the United States. I have lived in every time zone in the United States, so I think I might know a little more about the world than someone who has been in the same town for the last thirty years. Secondly if you lived by the same people, worked in the same job, and not traveled outside your state since you have been there, your worldly advice has a radius of about twenty miles. "Be careful where you stop to inquire for directions along the road of life." (Unknown, n.d.)

When giving advice, you have to know your audience. The supervisor of the mailroom cannot tell the CEO of the company how to run the company. They can share their ideas on how to improve procedures in the mailroom, but telling the CEO whether or not to invest in an overseas company may be out of their area of expertise. A commander of mine told us once "to stay in your lane." That meant everyone should do what they were hired to do or stick to what you do best for the company, and that is your job! This also included giving advice. I am not saying that you should not share ideas to make things better, but I am sure there are ways to do it better than giving unwanted advice.

People tend to take your advice a little more seriously if you are telling them something you actually went through that might be a little relevant to something they are going through or better yet if it is asked for by that person. Everyone has been through something that might help someone else. Like I said earlier, you have to know your audience and make sure it is relevant.

Getting Promoted is no Easy Task

Have you ever talked to someone who has made the statement that they could have made it to the rank of SGM but retired as an SFC? Did you ever ask them why did they only retire as an SFC if they thought they could have made SGM?

Don't let anyone fool you; getting promoted in the military is no easy task, especially to the senior ranks. You have about three to five senior officers and NCOs voting on thousands of records in a particular career management field in a month to select the best qualified for the next rank. The higher you go in rank, there are fewer slots to the next rank as well as less number of records they have to look at in order to choose the top Soldiers to be promoted. So, when someone says that they could have made the next rank but didn't, you have to ask yourself, well why didn't you? What secret formula do you know and why didn't you apply it to your career?

Don't get me wrong, people retire from the military for all different reasons, like they reached their goals, they are tired of moving, they want a change in their lifestyle, or they have an opportunity that they just cannot pass up. Whatever the reason, it is usually their choice. But adding to the reasoning that they could have made a higher rank is very misleading.

Getting promoted is like taking a test; the better you prepare for the test, the better you will do. Getting promoted is no different. You don't prepare to take the test the night before by doing an all-night cram session. You start preparing at the beginning of the class. You pay attention to the teacher along with what they are putting emphasis on, you ask questions to get a better understanding of the things that may be difficult to you, and you take the time to learn what is required to understand and pass the test. The same goes for getting promoted. It's all in the preparation, but it still doesn't mean you will make the score you want on the test or the rank you want to make. There could always be other factors that can cause you to get a lower score or not promoted. So, be careful when you are taking advice from those individuals.

Unless you know their story personally, they can or will tell you only what they want you to know. You have to look at the whole person and see where they are in their life and see if that's the person you wouldn't mine trading places with.

When I said earlier, people retire from the military for all different reasons, then you have to look at them to see if they are saying and doing the same things. Is their present situation better or worse? Are they having a tough time in their present job, don't have a job, or have a job that they are not happy in? Are they working to live or living to work? If the answers to those questions fall into the negative category, then you might want to be careful on taking advice from those particular individuals. They might fall in the category of they had to retire versus they wanted to retire. There is a difference.

See, both look the same on the exterior, but when you start to look under the surface, you will discover that there were other factors that could have caused them to retire early. They didn't prepare themselves to get promoted and they met their mandatory retirement date, they got in trouble and were forced to retire, or just couldn't get promoted. The longer you have been in the military, then you know what questions to ask—for example, how many years did you do? That could be one indicator because if they retired as an SFC and did twenty-four years, then that is one indicator that they probably met their mandatory retirement date. Another indicator is that they are always complaining about someone they knew made a higher rank than they did and keep harping on the fact that person shouldn't have made it. Another indicator could be the fact that they're always comparing all those "things" they did in their career that other people did and if they would have stayed in, then they would have been the same rank as that person. Those people are the ones that are usually bitter about how their careers turned out and can't let it go.

I don't want you to look at them from the prospective of material things that they have but from the fact of are they happy with their lives. If they have been retired for several years and are still talking about they could have made this rank or someone shouldn't have made that rank, in that case, they weren't satisfied with their careers and wanted more out of it. That is what I mean when I say don't take advice from someone you wouldn't trade places with. They are still looking for happiness and can't possibly tell you how to find that happiness in your career. The ones that always reflect on their careers as a happy time are usually the ones that were satisfied how their careers turned out. You don't hear them complaining about someone who was a thorn in their career or someone they know making to a higher rank than they did.

The military like any other business or organization in the fact that is not set up for everyone to get promoted to the highest positions. You can do all right things in the organization to put yourself in position to get promoted but still don't make it; it happens! But as long as you know that you did what you were supposed to do, then you just have to realize that things don't always turn out the way you wanted it to or expected it to turn out. That is life. You may not always reach your ultimate goals in life, but you just have to know that you prepared the best you could and you have to deal with the outcome.

You can deal with it one of two ways: always looking at it in the negative by living in the past or take that outcome and make the best out of it. Because that one door closes on you doesn't mean another won't open for you somewhere else. If your military career didn't go the way you wanted it to doesn't mean you don't have a chance to find satisfaction in your next career. As long as you are still living in the past, the present and future could pass you by, all so you wake up one day wondering what happen!

Relevance

Knowing how to work will ensure that you will always have a job; knowing why you work will ensure that you will be relevant in that job. There is a difference.

Were you relevant to the Army yesterday, are you relevant to the Army today, and most importantly, will you be relevant to the Army tomorrow?

If the Army's most valuable resources are America's sons and daughters, then how are you contributing to that value? Your relevance to the Army will describe how valuable of a resource you really are, a true diamond or cubic zirconium, 14K gold or fool's gold, crude oil or just crud.

Relevance is about what you bring to the Army or any organization for that matter. I would always ask my Soldiers, if you were taken out of the unit today, how would the unit function; the same, better, or worse? That is a sign of your relevance. I know we always say that everyone is replaceable and the mission will go on and of course it will, but the question is how proficiently will these things happen.

Were you relevant to the Army yesterday? Doubt will kill your dreams more than failure ever will because when most of us came into the Army, we probably did not have a clear path on what it took to get to the next level. Our first few years in, we were still trying to figure things out. As long as you were in the right place, at the right time, in the right uniform, then you were all right. The less your supervisor had to tell you, the more and more you started to become a valuable asset to your unit and the Army.

Once you started to figure things out on your own, then your value began to increase and your relevance began to show to your supervisor. Your responsibility started to increase and you were asked to do more. You were being selected to represent your platoon or unit. You were sent to various schools ahead of your peers. The next thing you knew, you were getting promoted and moving up in the ranks.

Are you relevant to the Army today? Never take advice from someone unless you are willing to trade places with because they are always the first ones to tell you how to succeed; in the meantime, they did not achieve that success. Everyone comes to work and does their job because that is what we get paid to do, and you cannot hang your hat on the fact that you are good at this or that. You should be good because that has been your job for ten plus years.

But, what new ideas are you bringing to the organization with all of your experience? Are you making sure that you are current with all the new trends you need to know for your existing position?

Will you be relevant to the Army tomorrow? Do not look behind you unless you are planning on going that way. Are you that person always talking about what you did at your last unit? A lot of people are afraid to leave their comfort zone. Try or do something new. So instead of embracing something new, you want to hold on to the past by saying that something will not work or it is a bad proposal without giving the new suggestion a chance to work.

When you try to stay in the past, then you will be left behind. You can always learn from the past hopefully not to make the same mistakes you or someone you know made to have a much-improved product. But when you live in the past, then you will not be able to see the future.

The world changes, viewpoints change, so why is it so difficult for you to change? In the Army, like any other organization, you have to deal with the culture of the organization. In order to change the organization, you have to change the culture in the organization.

A lot of times, we are so culturally conditioned that a little change is considered a threat to that organization's way of functioning. Instead of accepting the change to see if it is going to work, some people spend all of their energy trying to stop the change that they become unproductive or a hindrance to the organization.

If they would have used that same energy to embrace the change and give it a real chance of working, then they could have made an honest and informative assessment of the change to say that it would be a plus, equal, or minus for the organization.

How do we grow Leaders?

In a few conversations I had with some of the senior leaders I know, the topic of discipline always came up. After talking with many of our junior Soldiers, I see that we as leaders and NCOs have to do a better job setting the right example on and off duty. The standards you, as leaders, set will impact how Soldiers within your formation present themselves. We take care of Soldiers by holding them to a standard, which in turn will ensure we accomplish the mission. To understand how the standards and discipline are related you have to start with the basic premise of how we grow leaders in the Army. This is a three-step process.

Step one is establish a standard. The Army has plenty of Regulations, Pamphlets, Manuals, etc. that establish standards. Army Regulation 670-1, Wear and Appearance of the Army Uniform, is a standard that tells us how to wear items on the uniform and what accessories are authorized to wear on the uniform. The additional items we may wear on our uniforms—for example, access badges, or earplugs with our unit crest on the case—are standards set by the unit SOP.

Step two is to put someone in charge of enforcing the standards. This is where the leader is now responsible for his or her small piece of the Army. It may be two Soldiers or it may be ten. It is the leader who conducts daily inspections of Soldier's uniforms. It is the leader who conducts Pre-Combat Checks (PCC) of his or her Soldier's arms and equipment before going out on a mission. It is the leader who observes the Soldiers returning from a mission to ensure all have cleared their weapons to standards.

Step three, hold the leader accountable. This is where the more senior leaders have their responsibility. To see what is being done to standard, senior leaders have to inspect junior leaders. A Soldier who is missing a piece of equipment, means the leader missed this during the Pre-Combat Inspection (PCI) and obviously a more senior leader during the PCC.

So, for the more senior leaders, you must always remember your role in growing leaders. This leading by example empowers the leader to enforce standards on their small piece of the Army. It has always been said, when a more senior leader demonstrates a lesser standard, this demonstration now becomes the new standard. Enforcing basic standards and holding leaders accountable for their Soldiers is critical to developing these young leaders. Ask yourself, what does that lack of enforcement do to the success of your organization?

In every case where the leader stops enforcing fundamental standards and senior leaders do not hold him or her accountable, the enforcement of standards in other areas begins to slip. Shortcuts in performing Preventive Maintenance Checks and Services (PMCS) begin to become routine (a new standard), Soldiers stop wearing seat belts (a new standard), PCCs and PCIs are not performed in detail, complacency begins to set in, and leaders stop making on-the-spot corrections.

The importance of the squad, section, and platoon leadership in establishing standards and holding leaders accountable is critical to the success of the Army. When you walk into an organization or unit as an outsider and you should see everyone in the same uniform, basic fundamental drills performed as routine, everyone knows the standard, and you know that there is a leader in charge.

Marking Time versus Forward March

Complaining is just complaining, but complaining and doing something about it is called progression

I went to drill sergeant school in March of 1999. We had to learn a lot of modules to teach the new recruits how to march, salute, and the other basic positions while in formation. Marking Time is defined as a "military step in which Soldiers march in place, moving their legs as in marching, but without stepping forward. Forward March is defined as a regular, ordered, and synchronized walking of military formations." The Marking Time Soldier is the one that complains just to complain. The Forward March Soldier is the one that complains but does something about it.

You will find the Marking Time Soldier (not moving forward) no matter where you go or at whatever rank. They just sit around and complain about everything. No matter what you do for them, they are never happy. They complain about their assignment, their leadership, the unit, someone grading them wrong on their PT test, and the lists go on. They fall in that unwilling but able type of Soldier category. I would see that Soldier a lot when I went to a military school. They always wanted to complain about how the school was run but never offered any solutions to fix what they believed was the problem.

I was told once that you cannot fight your commander on every concern because you will be considered a nitpicker. Sometimes you have to let a few smaller problems go in order to fight for the bigger problems in the future. Your leadership will be more willing to listen to your issues if you don't protest and complain about every little thing that comes up. If you are the one that argues about everything, then most people begin to turn a deaf ear to you and you go unheard on issues that are most important to you.

The Marking Time Soldiers are very detrimental to a unit. They can cause a divide within the unit, which can sway the good order and discipline of the unit in a negative light. It can also have a pessimistic effect on the esprit de corps. As a leader, it is your responsibility and duty to make certain those types of Soldiers do not pollute the rest of the unit. The best way is continuous communication with your unit. The better informed your unit is, the less likely the Marking Time Soldier can taint the rest of the unit. You will never stop that Soldier from complaining or believing what they want to believe but the more you communicate the better you will have control of the situation. Daniel Patrick Moynihan said, "You're entitled to your own opinion. You're not entitled to your own facts." Hopefully, that Soldier began to realize that they are on an island and no one listens to them.

The Forward March Soldier (always moving forward) complains but does something about their complaints, which is called progression. Some people make things happen, while some people watch things happen, and you have people that wake up and wonder what happened. The Forward March Soldier is the one that makes things happen. This Soldier will tell you their issues and give you possible solutions to the issues. They understand that everything will not get fixed, but at least they had a chance to voice their opinion and it was taken into consideration. They move on to the next concern and continue to Soldier; this is your willing and able Soldier.

There are no perfect units in the Army. If the United States is the melting pot of the world, then the United States military is the melting pot of America. You will have a representation of America in your formations. You will have someone from every walk of life that you will have to deal with having all kinds of problems and concerns. As a leader, it is your job to curtail the issues. Be proactive and consistently working on your decision-making process will help you in the long run as a leader to deal with those situations.

Ultimate Professor

Coming into a job knowing one day it is going to end
One great thing about the military is that you have the opportunity to move to many different places, which means the opportunity to have many different duty positions. For me, this was a great thing because, at each duty station, I had a different position, which expanded my leadership abilities. This way you can go to your next duty position with new and fresh ideas to improve the operations of the unit. On the other hand, some people love what we call in the military "homesteading" because they are comfortable in their job, their spouse has a job they love, and their kids are in a great school, or whatever else is out there for a justification to stay at one duty station. If the leadership allows it, then that is their decision.

From my point of view, this can and will cause complacency within that duty position. The longer you stay in a certain position the less you begin to see. What I mean is this: you had been in that position so long that you got it down pat that when things around you begin to change, you cannot see it because you are still looking at the situation through the view you had when you first took the position. Everyone around you has changed, and you are the only constant, nevertheless you are in charge, causing you to miss the change in the unit, good or bad.

With new people, there will be changes because people come and go, which means new ideas come and go with them. But, if you come into a job knowing that it is going to end one day, you will not let complacency set in because you will set goals and have a timeline to get things done. You cannot let complacency be your way of life by staying in a job or position too long. You don't want to be labeled as "that guy."

We all know who "that guy" is. That is the individual who has been in the unit the longest and has not contributed anything to help the unit improve. That guy is the one who has been under three commanders and four first sergeants. That guy is the one that can tell you everything wrong with the unit but does not contribute to the success of the unit because they are too busy trying to tear the unit down. That guy is the one that has been in the unit so long they can tell you all the processes that have been tried in the unit and the ones that do not work. That guy is the one that always tries to get in good with the chain of command to make themselves look good, but as soon as the leadership is out of sight, so are they. That guy is the one that runs away from his/her duties and responsibilities. That guy is the one that always has an excuse for the reason why they are not getting promoted. That guy is the one that just walks around the unit bad-mouthing the leadership and saying they can do things better.

In order not to be labeled as that guy, you need to learn all you can while you are in that job and make it a point to leave that position when you become so comfortable in that job that things run better when you are not there. That should be your indicator that it is time to move on to something new. No matter what, it is going to end whether you want it to or not.

The Dash

There are two dates in everyone's life that are set in stone. The first one is the day you were born and the second is the day you pass. All of the other dates, like when you went to a school, permanent change of station (PCS), end of time of service (ETS), or Retire can always be a distant memory in someone's life or career. With that being said, the thing that is most important about those dates is the dash in the middle. That dash represents how you lived your life. How will you be remembered in your career? How did you affect other people lives?

That is the same thing every time you PCS to another duty station. Soldiers will not remember the day you arrived or the day you left. They will remember your dash. What you did or did not do for them while you were there. Were you a positive or negative influence on them? Did you provide purpose, direction, and motivation?

Everyone is a great leader in their own mind. I have not heard one person since I have been in the military that said that they were a bad leader. Well, I am here to tell you that you have some out there. Here is a test for you to determine if you meet the great leader category or not. Soldiers bring their problems to you because they have to; you are their supervisor.

The true sign of great leadership is when the Soldiers bring their problems to you when they do not have to bring you their problems. If you are not getting facebooked, twitted, or texted from your former Soldiers asking you for advice, then you may want to reevaluate your definition of a great leader.

It's difficult for many of us to ponder about our own afterlife, but the truth of the matter is that if we are to speculate what our lasting legacy will be, we must begin at the end of our lives. I think that's a fascinating reminder that, as leaders, we can dream, plan, and act on all of the things that we want our Soldiers to remember about us, or not. We are creating a legacy every day, whether or not we are deliberate about it.

Our ability to be humble reminds us that even the smallest, most apparently immaterial, or even insignificant things are the things our Soldiers will remember long after we are gone. Physical training sessions, deployments, field exercises, and organizational days, team building exercises, Sergeants Time Training, promotions, awards, and even counseling sessions—these are a pivotal part of what we will leave behind.

As I've given much thought to my own legacy, I've realized I don't want my Soldiers to remember me only as a shadow. The interactions we have to share with our Soldiers, shoulder to shoulder, is short and transient yet important.

I want the memories my Soldiers have of me to be connected and engaged. As we inject our legacy, let's aim to keep our hearts and minds fastened on that which will last. I always tell my NCOs and leaders that you must set the example by your actions, your appearance, demonstrating your tactical and technical knowledge, and by taking an honest interest in their well-being and the well-being of their families.

This is the very significant in my unit because they are the Soldier's appointed leaders. They should take that leadership and cherish it with their life. They look to them for direction and guidance. So, provide that direction and guidance and require of them no more or less than you would require of yourself.

When I was a junior Soldier and NCO, and had to go to my senior Officers' and NCOs' offices for whatever reasons, I would look at their walls, desks, and bookshelves and see all of their pictures, guidons, swords, sabers, and other knickknacks. I would think to myself that they were great leaders to receive all of those accolades from their former Soldiers, then I became a leader only to find out what those artifacts were really about.

Everyone who was in a leadership position, good or bad, received those kinds of things just for being there. You know a token of the unit's appreciation for taking care of their needs, so to speak, while they were the leadership. As I started to move up in rank, I realized that those trinkets were nice to have and great for telling stories, but did they really tell the story of how you took care of your Soldiers by the gift you received leaving the unit?

For me and me only, the more I moved up in rank, the more I realized that I was the proudest when I heard someone I didn't know using one of my aphorisms or what the Soldiers like to call "Hargroveisms." I would ask them about it and more often than not say they got it from sergeant so-and-so, who usually turned out to be one of my former Soldiers. That would gratify me more than any souvenir I had received from my Soldiers from my previous assignments.

I think that should be your reward when you know that you got through to your Soldiers where they are repeating to their Soldiers the same things you told them. Please, don't get me wrong, I appreciated them thinking of me with a gift. Typically, when it comes to tokens of appreciation or awards, people get wrapped up in who has received what and at the end of the day, most of us have similar things anyway.

On the other hand, if you see your Soldiers believing in you so much that they are emulating you to their Soldiers, then that should be an honor you should cherish for the rest of your life. It is kind of like saying or doing the same things to your kids that your parents said and did to you when you were the same age. At that time, you may not have liked it, but you got the picture.

As a leader, my reward had been when my Soldiers got what they deserved as far as a promotion, award, or a school that they wanted. A lot of leaders do not understand that if your Soldiers succeed, then you will routinely succeed; they go hand in hand. Trying to suppress their development will only hurt your progression in the long run. If you ensure they get theirs, yours will come in the end.

I was talking with one of my commanders one day after the sergeants major list was released, and he told me that he couldn't believe that I wasn't on it. I told him not worry about it because I did not compete. He was shocked and said that was fine for me and my career if I decided not to compete for the next rank, but what about my NCOs who kept seeing me getting passed over for promotion. I never would ever tell them that I didn't compete for sergeant major because I would stay on their case about always being ready to compete for the next rank, but I wasn't. He asked me what are they to think to see me doing all the right things but not getting promoted. He had me thinking about it for a second, but I had to tell him that I have more work to do as a first sergeant, and when they get to the next level, then I will get promoted. I smiled at him because he had the same shocked look on his face because of my statement.

The following sergeant first class list came out, and five out of my six eligible staff sergeants made the list. So my work was done, and I was on the following sergeants major list. I am not saying that what I did got them promoted, but I wanted to make sure that I put them in certain situations by making sure they were in the best possible position in their careers to achieve the next level. When they were, my work was done, and I received my rewards and accolades. How will your dash be remembered as the leader?

Unapproachable
Adjective (Merriam-Webster, 1828)
   1. not approachable: physically inaccessible
   2. discouraging intimacies: reserved

I have been in the Army for a total of thirty years, and I have always heard the phrase "People think that I am not approachable or that person is unapproachable." At first, I never seriously thought about it and just went on about my business. When one of my CSM said she was unapproachable, then I took the time to think truly about what it meant to be unapproachable. Websters online defines unapproachable *"as not approachable, physically inaccessible, discouraging intimacies, or reserved."* Thinking back to her, I am assuming she was thinking of herself as the physically inaccessible (hard to find) definition because the others did not match. She was never there.

Well, here is my theory about the word unapproachable and how it applies to people. Most people are not an intimidating force that you have to be scared or afraid of because they are not going to harm or kill you. One thought is people who are unapproachable are more likely unreasonable and not unapproachable. When you talk to them, you already know what you are going to get from that person. Some negative response or whatever the situation, their minds are already made-up.

Now, I have run into a lot of those people, and it was just hard to start a conversation with them about anything. You talk to them because you have to and then you keep the conversation as short as possible.

Another unapproachable person is the one that has to put themselves in every situation. For example, they did this or that: they did it better, or no matter what the situation, they always seem to express what they did or "I was that" in the core of what was going on at that time. You always get turned off by those people because the conversation always seems to end up about them. As a leader, your subordinates want to know what you are going to do for them today and tomorrow and not what you did in the past for yourself.

An additional unapproachable person is the one that thinks they are smarter than everyone else in the room and always tries to prove it. It is okay to be rational or be the subject matter expert on something, but most people get turned off when that person continually throws it up in their face that they are smarter than you and is always trying to prove it with every single situation. I always say "it is not bragging when you can back it up" but you can turn people off when your confidence turns into cocky, over-bearing, or arrogance. It is not for you to decide, but when people would rather be uninformed on a subject than to seek your advice, then you might be that unapproachable person.

People like to use the word unapproachable as a cop-out. They know what kind of person they are, so instead of dealing with their faults, they throw the word unapproachable out to justify how they are with the rest of the world. Doing an honest self-assessment and making an attempt to correct your short-comings will reduce the number of unapproachable people in the Army.

"The less you associate with some people, the more your life will improve. Any time you tolerate mediocrity in others, it increases your mediocrity. An important attribute in successful people is their impatience with negative thinking and acting people. As you grow, your associates will change. Some of your friends will not want you to go on to bigger and better things. They will want you to stay where they are…. Friends that don't help you climb will want you to crawl. Your friends will stretch your vision or choke your dream. Those that do not increase you will eventually decrease you." (Powell, n.d.)

So always be on the lookout for those so-called unapproachable people. The simple but true fact of life is that you become like those with whom you closely associate—for the good and the bad.

Leadership: Taught or Born with it?

I am who I am! This means that I am the same person I was ever since I joined the military. I have adjusted a few things or two, but overall, I am still the same person. On the other hand, the military has taught me lifelong skills that include leadership; so, is it taught, or you are born with it? To lead is easy, but your decision-making process is what makes leadership hard. How do you handle situations?

I will always say that leadership is nothing more than confidence in your abilities and who you are as a person, your personality. That is what separates the CSM from the SGT. Confidence! The more you move up in rank, the more confidence you have in your abilities. I want you to think about something. When you were junior in rank, how many times did you walk past someone (usually of higher rank) that needed an on-the-spot correction and you said nothing to that Soldier. It could be for a number of reasons, like you did not see the violation, you saw it but did not know the regulation that covers that situation, or you just did not know how the senior was going to react, and you did not have the confidence to confront that person.

I have been going back and forth with this question: "Is leadership taught or are you born with it?" For me, your personality shapes your leadership. We have all been to the same leadership schools but still we all come out of them with something different, why? We all take the same tests, read the same coursework, and perform the same tasks.

Nevertheless, we all have different ways of learning like some do better by seeing, others do better by doing, while others do better by reading. One reason is that it might be based on your personality because we are human. We all act differently to different situations because of a lot of different factors like your thinking process, your experiences, or how you view things.

On the other hand, the question should be "what determines your leadership?" Out of my thirty years in the Army, leadership is determined by the people you are with and in charge of at that time because the individual you help or did not help will determine if you are a leader or not. Like the saying goes "your reputation will precede you" and that is so true because where do you get the reputation you have in your career?

The people you have served with are the ones that make or break your reputation. It is like when you were dating in high school; well, the people you date become your mouthpiece for the good or bad. How you treat them will become your dating reputation because they have to tell someone and it will spread if you want it to or not. So, the same is true about leadership; your reputation will make you a great, good, or bad leader. You can ask three different Soldiers that you served with at the same time and get three different responses because of what you did or did not do for them.

Leadership has nothing to do with what school you did or did not attend but how well your decision-making process is and how you handle situations. Also, your subordinates will see how much you will fight for them especially in a bad situation. Let us look outside of the military for a minute and who have been labeled as great leaders or someone you have called a great leader. A lot of people in different career fields come to mind like a quarterback on a football team, a CEO of a big corporation, or someone who leads a movement to get things changed. So, if that is true, I have not seen a lot of them in our military leadership schools.

Do not get me wrong, you can always get a pearl or two when you go to those schools, but they do not shape who you are as a leader. If that were or is the case, then why do not we all make the same decisions when it comes to situations. I will tell you why, and that is that your decisions are based on your experience, personality, and what is in the lines of the law as you see them. Your interpretation of something will be different to how other leaders see things. This is why leaders make different decisions on the same issue.

The thing you have to do as a leader is to get everyone in your footprint going in the same direction and trust that you can take them there. That is the hardest thing to do because you have to mold all those different personalities together to function as one.

I always ask this scenario of my NCOs—you come into the unit, and you are assigned a squad of ten and they all hate each other and cannot get along. You have all types from all walks of life. How do you get them to function as one? I have heard everything from taking them out to eat to holding a sensing session to a team building exercise. There are no wrong answers, as I was saying earlier; we all make different decisions regarding the same issues. The difference is how long it will take one leader from another to get them to function as one. "If you are going to achieve excellence in big things, you develop the habit in little matters." (Powell, n.d.)

Contrary to popular belief, leadership is not liker-ship. Obtain the respect of your Soldiers. Their personal devotion is very desirable, but can only be gained by treating your Soldiers fairly, justly, and impartially. You must set the example by your actions, your appearance, demonstrating your tactical and technical knowledge, and by taking an honest interest in their well-being and the well-being of their families. You are their appointed leader. Take that leadership and cherish it with your life. They look to **you** for direction and guidance. So, provide that direction and guidance and require of them no more or less than you would require of yourself. Do not drive your Soldiers or stand on the sidelines watching them…. **Lead Them!!**

There are a lot of leadership characteristics that define a leader and many of them that can be taught like being a good communicator, learning good organizational skills, understanding how to delegate, or utilizing the resources available to you. Nevertheless, the desire to lead people and the willingness to motivate your subordinates is something that cannot be taught. This characteristic is something that is internal to each individual; you can't learn it in a leadership school or an eight-hour class.

This quality is what separates the good leaders from the great leaders. The great ones have that aspiration to want constantly to lead along with making the ones around them better. If you don't have that longing to make yourself better as well as the people around you better, all the classes in the world won't make you a great leader.

Scores of people describe this quality as having heart, mentally strong, or even being focused. No matter what it's called, it all boils down to one thing, and that is they don't let doubt, failure, or a defeatist attitude stop them from achieving their goals. Michael Jordon isn't the greatest basketball player of all time based on his talent alone.

What separated him from all the others was his desire to be the best. Most of us have read or heard of him always trying to improve on his skills, furthermore having the willingness to do it. Every other player that was going to play against him knew that they were going to get his best every time they played him. He didn't care if you were the star of the team or the twelfth man on the team; you were going to get all he had whenever he stepped on the court.

If you look at sports as a whole, what separated the ones that just wanted to make the team to the ones that made it to the Hall of Fame in their particular sport? It wasn't just their talent but their willingness and desire to be the best! Either you have it or you don't.

Trust but Verify

Many times we put our trust in people we previously knew. Leadership has to do with trust; the trust your subordinates have in you and trust you should have in your subordinates. When you come through the ranks, you make friendships with people that you hope would last a lifetime. Many of them do, but you have some friendships that last for only that moment in time.

When you were younger, you met people that had the same general interest you had when you met, and you enjoyed each other's company. Some people grow while others stay at that same moment in time. So, when you meet up with that person again, you find out that you are not the same people you were when you first met. I have seen this many times in the military.

You may have met someone in basic training or at your first duty station and become close friends. In the military, we move to many different duty stations during our careers and may not see that person for a few years or even if at all. But maybe after a couple of moves, you run into that person again only to find out that one has matured, and the other is still the same person when they first met.

The problem starts when one is the supervisor and the other is the subordinate. Both tend to think there will not be a problem because they were friends in the past. But the problem is one will see the relationship how it was while the other will see it how it is now. Neither one will see at first that people change over the years.

We all change as the years goes by. Some people realize they want more out of life while others still enjoy the life they lived when they were younger. When you see someone that you have not been in contact with or seen over a few years, you tend to see that person how they were when you knew them and not how they are now.

We all do it, and some take longer than others to realize that the relationship has changed for better or worse depending on if you are the supervisor or the subordinate. So, as leaders, when do you end your friendship and start your leadership? When I was a 1SG in Germany, I had such a situation.

I wanted to see this person as I saw them when we were stationed together a long time ago. When I knew this NCO, they were very squared away (a statement we use in the military that says they are very good at what they do). When this NCO came to me, I put her in one of the most important positions in the unit, operations NCO.

I was a First Sergeant, and she was a Staff Sergeant. When we were stationed together a few years earlier, we both were Sergeants. I still saw her as the NCO I knew, so that is why I wanted her as the operations NCO, big mistake. Instead of me looking at her as the person she was now, I tried to put her in this position thinking that she would take the position, and I wouldn't have to worry about her performance when she was as the person I knew before.

She always had a reason she couldn't attend a field training exercise and never completed a task that was given to her. After about six months, I had to replace her with a more junior NCO who performed remarkably. If I had kept her in this position based on our friendship, both of us would have been out of a job.

Friendships go a long way, and you want to make sure that if you are in a position to help them, you should. But if they are not able or willing to perform at a level you need them to for the position you put them in, then you need to let them go. Sometimes that is the best way to preserve the friendship.

You can put them in a position that they can handle, and you don't have to look like you're playing favorites by continuing to let that person under-perform just to maintain the bond you have established. As a leader, you have to know the difference and not let one outweigh the other just to hold on to a past relationship that, in the long run, will not matter to you in the future.

Be Your Own Person

No matter who is your mentor, what book you read, or similar situation you were in, you have to be your own person. I don't care how hard you try, there will only be this person or that person, and there will never be the next somebody else. I know it is human nature to compare this person to that person or say such-and-such would have handled it differently; well they should because we are all different. The faster you learn that, as a leader, the better it will be for you.

We are defined by who we are and not what we are. In the military, people like to define you by your MOS or branch. Your ability to handle a situation comes much later or by an unusual set of circumstances. When you first meet someone, and through the process of general conversations, your job comes up and in an instant no matter what you have done before or what you are doing now, you are automatically grouped as a person they knew before in that same job or career management field (CMF).

It is so unfortunate that you are dealt with that way, but that is the environment we live within the military. Instead of basing your leadership ability on the jobs you had previous, the situations, you have been in, and what you are currently doing now.

Once you show someone that you are a good leader, the next thing that comes out of someone's mouth is "I have never met a squared away this or that." Really, like you have met all the people in that particular career field and every one of them has failed at everything they have done in their career up to the point where they met you. You may even be the same rank or outrank that person with that ridiculous thought process.

I was about a month or two from graduation from the sergeants major academy when we received our orders. The division CSM and a few of the BDE CSMs of the division I was going to came to the academy for a meet-and-greet. It was about fifteen of us headed to this particular division. We all met in one of the conference rooms, and the division CSM started going through his agenda. He was asking questions like who deployed, family issues, and the normal protocol we as leaders do in the military. Then he started talking to individuals, when he turned to me and asked me about being dental. Then he asked the room "what was he going to do with me," then he said, "He guesses you could do dental readiness." I stood up and told him that I was a Zulu (all sergeants major based on their CMF) and dental readiness is done by Sergeants.

I arrived in Hawaii and got bounced around from BDE to BDE. Finally, one of the deployed BDEs stated to the division CSM that they needed me downrange. It took me about two weeks to get ready to deploy, and I deployed. Once again, they really didn't know what to do with me because they were basing their decisions on my former job and not what I could bring to the table. I was confident in my abilities, and I had been through this before, so I just relaxed and waited until the decision was made where to put me. I was placed with the stability transition team (STT).

We were responsible for helping the Iraqis transition to a stable country after the war. I stayed true to whom I was and was my own person. I went from the dental sergeant major in the beginning of the deployment to just sergeant major by the end of the deployment with a job offer to become the operations sergeant major for one of the battalions.

You have to be who you are because trying to be someone else will only last for a small amount of time, and the true you will eventually come out. If I were trying to be someone else, I would have failed. You take on any challenge that comes your way, but the difference for each and every challenge is that you will put your own personal spin on whatever it is you know, taking ownership. Once you do that and are comfortable in your own skin, you will succeed no matter what obstacle is put in front of you.

Identity Thief

We have a problem in the world today which is called identity theft. That is when an individual takes your private information and uses it for their personal business. We have the same problem in the Army, identity theft. It is not the one that I just spoke about but the one when somebody tries to be someone they are not. The only person you can be is the one you see in the mirror every day. You cannot be the next anybody else. You hear this all the time in sports where the media and fans try to compare a former player with a current player.

Well, in the Army, it is a little different. You have Soldiers trying to be their mentors or someone they knew from a previous assignment. I didn't say "trying to be like" but be that person and take on their leadership style because it works. It is okay to take some leadership characteristics from someone, but taking their whole persona will backfire on you every time.

You are an original and so is the person that you are trying to be. No one knows you better than you. When you show that facade and people find out that what you presented is not the real you, how do you think they will take you then?

We all have someone that crossed our paths that we enjoyed being around for different reasons—for example, they are funny, they have a way of explaining things, people just flock to them, or in your eyes they always make all the right decisions. Well, whatever the reason, it is that person, how they are and not who you are.

Like I said earlier, it is okay to take things from them, but you are not them. If you like how someone handles a certain situation, then it is okay for you to see the process and follow how that person went about handling the issue, but it is not okay for you to transform yourself into that person and do it exactly how they did it. You have to discover your own leadership style and the way of handling things.

Being someone else will only last for so long before the real you comes out. You will not be able to keep up the charade because of someone that might know you from a previous experience or a situation that might bring out the actual you.

Granny Hargrove told me a long time ago to play the game in the uniform and the equipment that was issued to you. That means you have your own brain, personality, and looks, so you are not going into the world with any less than someone else. Trust in your abilities; you might surprise yourself on what you are able to accomplish!

Deflection - let me take the negativity off of me and place the negative light on you

When you want to see the true character of someone, see how they react in a time of adversity. Many people, when they are getting an award or receiving praise, like to stand proudly alone, with their chest out thinking they did it on their own. On the other hand, when those same people are in trouble, they want to bring everyone down with them. Blaming everyone else for their dilemma, and it is called deflection. I am going to call you a bad leader before you can call me a bad subordinate.

When you are in a leadership position, weird people have the propensity to come after you from all perspectives. Deflection is one of the most common ways to divert attention from themselves to the ones that are in those leadership positions.

Deflection occurs when that substandard individual calls or accuses you of negativity before you can do it to them. To get the focus off of them, when people get in trouble, they like to start placing blame on the leadership. They have a tendency to make statements about how the leadership did not take care of their needs or how they are doing them wrong when all along it is them that is in the wrong.

I have seen the scenario play out many times just with different characters. Most of the time the person is already a subpar individual and it will be just a matter of time before they are on their way out of the organization. They continue to stay in trouble, and when the final straw is broken that is when they go into a deflection mode by blaming everyone else and not taking responsibility for their own actions.

No one was there when they got into trouble, but when they get caught, they will tell anyone who will listen how everyone else is at fault. This gains them time to use what little resources they have left to figure a way out or at least minimize the punishment they are about to receive.

The most prevalent time in my career that I saw the most cases of deflection is when I was a Drill Sergeant. Being a Drill Sergeant was an honor and you had to have performed well in the operational Army to be selected to be a Drill Sergeant. I was selected to be a Drill Sergeant a few years after the Army had a big crisis with Drill Sergeant and leadership during basic combat training; it was a tough time to be a Drill Sergeant for a few years to come.

The Soldiers that came into the Army during that time were ignorant to the Army but not to life. The new recruits received briefing after briefing from the leadership, to the IG, and EO about if anyone is doing something to them that they feel is inappropriate that they had direct access to them.

There are always some leaders that will do the wrong thing. but for the most part leaders in actuality try to do the right thing. With this direct access to everyone in the Army, the Soldiers use it to their advantage. The leadership took everything the Soldiers would say and you would find yourself defending everything you'd said or done. They would fill out their assessments and what they said about you carried a lot of weight.

So, when the Soldiers would get in trouble is where you would see the deflection. You would find yourself defending your actions rather than the Soldiers being reprimanded for their bad behavior while the other Soldiers would see this, which made it hard to be a somewhat effective leader. A lot of them got away with the bad behavior, and it was carried with them to their permanent duty stations where things were a little different.

The best way to deal with deflection is to make sure you do not give that subpar person anything to negotiate with or something they can use against you. As a leader, your character is on display 24/7/365 and people will always look for anything in your DNA that they may use against you later.

Do not give them ammo that they are looking for so they can shoot you with it in the future. I am not asking you to be perfect, but just make sure that you are doing the right thing all the time and you should not have too much to worry about.

If I handed you the keys to a Porsche,
all you have to do is drive it and try not to wreck it
When I was the 1SG in Germany, I came into the unit where there were things that needed to be fixed immediately. The main body of the unit deployed and the rear detachment had their so-called "own" way of doing things. The first morning I was going to do PT with the unit, I saw one of their own ways of doing things. It was a Monday morning, and all the Soldiers came to PT in civilian clothes because they were on their way to the gym. I thought it was a special day, organization day, or a fun day. Therefore, I really did not say anything until I saw that same thing the next day.

I immediately approached the rear detachment NCOIC and asked him what he was doing, but before he could get it out, I made all the Soldiers change into the proper uniform so we could conduct PT. The rest of the day did not go any better after I finished my in-processing and went to the unit for my first official day.

Rest assured, after I had left that unit four years later, the unit was running like a newly tuned-up Porsche because I put a lot of time and energy into that unit so it could function better when I am not there. So, I told the incoming 1SG that I am handing you the keys to this Porsche, all you have to do is drive it and try not to wreck it, during my change of responsibility ceremony.

Many times leaders come into a situation and try to change things without doing an assessment to see what needs to be fixed or just left alone. You do not always have to come in and change things just because you are in charge. If some things are working fine, maybe sometimes it is the leader that needs to adjust to the situation instead of the other way around.

We are so quick to put our stamp on some things that we do not see it may already be working fine the way it is or just maybe small adjustments. Because one thing works in one place like your previous unit doesn't always equate that it is going to work everywhere.

The situation is different no matter how you try to relate it to your prior one, and as a leader you need to recognize the differences. No two units or situations are the same, so that should be an indicator that sometimes it is you that needs to change. Even if you return to a unit that you were previously in, it will not be the same because the people you knew there have changed, which mean the situation for all intents and purposes has changed.

Not all change is good or welcome so that is why doing a proper assessment of your situation is so vital. You do not want to come into an organization, be so quick to make changes that may not be needed, and have the organization starting to question your competence before you really have a chance to prove your true worth.

This is like trust; hard to earn but easy to lose. That can be said about the negative or unneeded change. Why are you making arbitrary changes without reason? "Just because" is not an answer because you will lose your support within the organization, and it will be difficult to get back.

When you are coming into a situation, do a proper assessment to see what you have and see what you need. Asked the questions of why things are done in a certain way. If the answers do not make since or the famous "just because" for you to make a change, then let your leadership take over and by all means make that needed change for the better. If the answers make sense and are unique to that organization for you to keep things the way they are, then a change may not be needed at that particular time. Do not let pride and your feelings give you the need to put your stamp of approval on everything that would affect the overall success of the unit and your position.

Teaching is mostly about listening, and learning is mostly about talking
"When you control a man's thinking you do not have to worry about his actions. You do not have to tell him not to stand here or go yonder. He will find his 'proper place' and will stay in it. You do not need to send him to the back door. He will go without being told. In fact, if there is no back door, he will cut one for his special benefit. His education makes it necessary." Carter G. Woodson

No matter if you are teaching a pre-kindergarten class, college-level students, or Senior Noncommissioned Officers, a teacher's job is to inspire their students beyond their level of their own academic achievement. Leaders are the teachers in their chosen profession. If you are a true teacher, then your job is to pass along your knowledge to the ones that are coming behind you. You cannot take it with you, so the best thing you can do is pass it to the future leaders in your field. You have to be careful whom you try to teach.

Everyone has their own apex in life where they are ready to learn what it takes to get to the next level. As a teacher, you need to know this because if you are trying to pass the mantle of knowledge to someone who is not ready to receive it, then you might have wasted valuable time instead of trying to teach someone who is ready to learn. How do you know when someone is ready?

Well, most of the time, they will tell you they are ready to learn by asking questions. Once the question had been asked, then you should be in full-receive mode only. The student will ask you what they want to know. If you waste their time trying to teach them things they might not want to know or know at that time, you might lose that student. You need to listen to that student because they might know more than what you give them credit for knowing. You want them to feel at ease talking to you and for you not to talk at them but listen with an attentive ear.

The more you get them to talk, the more you know about that student and what level of instruction is required for that particular student. If you carry the conversation, then you will limit the student's wiliness to be taught.

Not everyone in the world learns in the same manner so why should you teach or be taught in the same way? Academic freedom is a way to allow teachers the freedom to get the subject matter across to their students in the best manner they can to achieve the desired goal of educating their students.

As a coach, teacher, and mentor in the Army, I use a variety of methods to ensure my Soldiers get the objective of the lesson or task at hand. Some people learn by listening to others, while some learn by watching, and yet some learn by doing. You should use either method or a combination of all three.

As a student, academic freedom was always encouraged where I went to school. Critical thinking was always part of the subject matter. Not only what was the right answer but how did you come up with the answer. Academic freedom is about knowing when to complicate the students thinking by presenting them with opinions they have not thought about and when to let their own thinking take over. Academic freedom is allowing students to make mistakes so the teacher can assess the students understanding of a subject and how a student's mind is working. That is where the real learning takes place.

Everyone must know the classroom's vision and goals. The best practices must be able to articulate and reinforce that to be a successful classroom. One best practice is that you must give your students clear goals and what you expect of them as students. When people know what is expected of them and goals they have to reach, then there should not be any misunderstanding when it comes to classroom performance. That goes into the next best practice of communication.

Communication is one of the most important but misused skill set. Most people assume that they communicate their ideas clearly to someone but do not ask for feedback to ensure that their points were received in the way it was intended. Honest evaluations are probably the hardest best practice. Everyone wants to hear when they are doing great but are not receptive when they are doing badly. A lot of teachers have a tough time telling someone the truth when it comes to classroom performance. No one wants to be the bad guy. In order to achieve the classroom's goals and vision, everyone must be working in the same direction.

Classrooms are environments promoting individual and team learning capabilities. Teachers continue to strive to build classrooms that improve effectiveness, and possess an ability to continuously evolve. Classrooms depend on effective communication; a chief component of leadership influence. They also require thinking from as many perspectives as possible, in order to evolve and grow in response to anticipated and actual external pressures. These perspectives emerge from experience diversity. Thus, teachers must recognize the value of a diverse classroom as an important resource in a classrooms' ability to learn and manage change.

Leadership Development

Leadership development is a continual learning process. It is influenced not only externally by things that happen to us (e.g., we attend military schools, we serve through a sequence of assignments such as platoon sergeant, first sergeant, staff, etc.), but also is affected by things we do for ourselves. In this way, leadership development is partly internally influenced. In other words, there are specific leadership activities we can decide to engage in and from which we can learn. As developing leaders, we can choose who we learn from, which situations we place ourselves in and, for the most part, what and how we learn.

After you have found you a mentor, the next thing you should do is to do a **TRUE** self-assessment. What I mean by a true self-assessment is to look yourself in the mirror and determine what you need to improve on. A lot of people may say that they know you, but the only person that really knows you is you! You can fool some of the people all the time and all the people some of the time, but you can't fool yourself any of the time. You know your true strengths and weaknesses, and if you don't take the time to develop those strengths and improve those weaknesses, then you will not grow as a leader. I always did my leadership development during my birthday month so I wouldn't forget and I know it was a full year since I did my last one.

First, ask your seniors, peers, and subordinates to give you an honest evaluation. The Army's 360-degree assessment is a good tool to use because it allows you to send out the assessment to your seniors, peers, and subordinates. The assessment is sent out to people so they can give you their assessment of you as a leader. It can ask them to rate you on your leadership style, values, morals, and anything else that can positively or negatively impact you as a leader.

One common mistake people make is that they send it only to the ones that will give them a great review. In order to get a true and fair assessment, you want to send it to people you know that may not have a great opinion of you. I am not saying send it to a person that you had a major problem with because their opinion could be one-sided in the opposite direction and you won't get any value out of it. Instead, send it to people that you have contact with but not necessary think of you in any particular way. There are other types of assessment you can do, just find one to fit your needs.

Second, continue to work on your Individual Development Plan (IDP). An IDP is an individual plan you come up with to help you reach your goals. There are a many different ones out there, but they are basically the same. Usually, the IDP has things like career goals, personal goals, development needs, success inhibitors, and primary strengths.

Career goals can be broken down as desired next position(s) in the short term and long term. Personal goals can be pursuit of higher education or degree completion, spending more time with family, or working on your spiritual needs. Development needs should identify the key strengths that should be further developed or any gaps in behaviors, skills, or attributes needed to ensure success at the next level. Success inhibitors can address objective and measurable negative behaviors that could keep the individual from fully utilizing their strengths and may negatively impact their success or potential career advancement. Primary strengths should clearly identify the characteristics that differentiate your leadership from others in the organization.

Third, is to develop your Leadership Develop Action Plan (LDAP). The LDAP helps develop your strengths and improve your weaknesses. This plan is what and how we learn by motivating, decision-making, planning, execution, assessing, developing, and learning.

Learning involves an essential shift or progress of the mind where creation is evident and enjoins activities such as re-engineering, envisioning, changing, adapting, moving into and creating the future. Seek and generate additional challenges and let your leaders know you are looking for increased responsibility and personal growth. Focus on your learning priorities by keeping a list of things you want to learn during the next three months, year, three years, and five years. Show this list to your mentor and develop a plan that involves continuing effort. Make some form of public commitment to your learning goals so others will encourage you to reach them. Show your goals to others, talk about them, and post them where you'll be reminded daily. Share your mistakes by talking through the mistake with others you trust. This will often increase your understanding of the situation. Solicit their input regarding what you might do differently in the future. Openly discussing mistakes will increase learning and can help build the organization through developing trust.

Developing embraces the art of teaching, training, coaching, and counseling subordinates to increase their knowledge, skills, and confidence. We develop the competence and self-confidence of subordinate leaders through role modeling and/or training and having them engage in developmental activities related to their current or future duties. Stay alert for articles, news reports, and media information that might be useful to others. Discuss them with peers or subordinates and pass them on. Lead a discussion with subordinates or peers regarding the organization of your higher headquarters. Use a copy of the organizational chart and assign people to explain the major functions of other units within the command. Have the group identify areas of interdependence, support, and effects on your unit's mission.

Assessing refers to effectively and appropriately using evaluation tools to facilitate continual improvement. Communicate your standards and expectations before any event, activity, or performance that you deem worthy of assessment.

Become proficient at assessing individual NCO performance. Study and become familiar with the NCO-ER and how to write correct and influential reports. Write an example of what you think would be a great report, a moderately successful report, and a weak report. Do these before you write actual reports.

Execution comprises the ability to complete individual and unit assigned tasks according to specified standards and within certain time criteria or event criteria. Promote aggressiveness and initiative in subordinates by allowing them to execute as they see fit within your broadly defined intent. Informally and periodically ask your subordinates, "What can I do to help you be more effective?" Show openness and listen carefully to what they tell you.

Planning (and organizing) establishes a course of action for oneself and others to accomplish goals. Planning establishes priorities and appropriately allocates time and resources (to include people). Find out which of your peers is considered to be a good tactical planner. Shadow this person as they conduct the planning process. Consult with skilled planners; observe and ask about their planning process; review their written plans; observe their tracking systems; and ask them to give feedback regarding your plans. Ask a trusted peer to play "devil's advocate" by confronting you with all possible things that could go wrong with your plan. Make appropriate changes and contingency plans for issues that are uncovered.

Decision-making constitutes the ability to react to information and the readiness to take appropriate actions based on the sound, logical conclusions based on an analysis of fact. Resist making "snap" decisions when time is available. Do the following when presented with your next problem: define the problem and take time to generate. Make wise use of existing information when considering your decision.

Successful decision-makers often look to the past and to others to determine what might be the best course of action. Talk with other leaders who might have worthwhile information regarding your issue. Seek out leaders who have dealt with the same issue and learn from what they've done. Stop yourself from pushing your decision-making responsibilities upward. Take problems to your superior only when you have exhausted your ability to solve the problem. Provide your superior with background information and a recommendation. Take ownership of your decision and those of your superiors.

Motivating embodies using an individual's desires and needs to influence how he thinks and what he does. Motivating uses appropriate incentives and methods to reinforce individuals or groups as they effectively work toward task accomplishment and resolution of conflicts and disagreements. Coupled with influence, motivating involves empowering subordinate leaders to achieve organizational goals and properly rewarding their efforts as they achieve the goals. Get to know your subordinates and their needs. What rewards are important to them? What motivates them? Be creative in rewarding positive performance. Make a daily habit of catching people doing something right and reinforce them. Praise can be a powerful motivator. Instead of looking for mistakes to punish, focus on finding examples of desirable behavior and then use praise to reinforce it quickly.

Remember, the higher you climb the flagpole, the more your rear shows. Self-improvement is a process; it's more like a marathon than a sprint. The only thing that is consistent is change. If you don't change with the times, then you will be left behind. Doing things the way you used to do it and you are not achieving the results that you want, then you are the problem.

We have a saying in the Army, "Continue to improve your foxhole!" That means never think your fighting position is good enough. There is always something you can do to get a better advantage over your adversaries. Why not take that same mindset when it comes to your leadership development? Your adversaries can be anything from not taking the hard jobs that will help your career, not trying to improve on your weaknesses, or not accepting the fact that the world is changing around you.

There is not a magic formula or blueprint that says that you will move forward in your career because if there were, then everyone would make it to the senior levels. However, not doing anything to improve your current circumstances is a guaranteed way to ensure you won't go as far as you may want to in the Army or life for that matter. Regardless, how you do it, you must continue to look for ways to improve your foxhole.

Lessons Learned

1. There are four kinds of Soldiers—willing and able, willing and unable, unwilling and able, unwilling and unable. NCOs need to know how to lead each and which one are you?

The willing and able Soldier is the one that you just give them a task and get out of their way. The only thing you have to do is come back to check on their progress. This type of Soldier is truly only about 10 to 15 percent of the Army. The reason the number is so low is because a lot of people have a hard time separating the true willing and able Soldier who can also be described as a selfless service Soldier from the ones who are just self-serving. The willing and able Soldier will succeed and ensuring their Soldiers and peers around them succeed. They are not afraid to share information because they know it is not just about them but about the **TEAM** (Together Everyone Achieves More). They also know that it is not about what someone else does in their career but more importantly what they do in their own career. They understand that if they do what they are supposed to do, they will progress in their career. The ones who are just self-serving will concern themselves more about what they are going to get out of the deal than if they help the ones around them. They will do things for others as long as they receive some form of accolades in the process. They have the tools to be a true willing and able Soldier, but their judgment becomes cloudy when they think someone will pass them up or have more than what they have in their military records. The self-serving Soldier is not all bad because they will help others, but it begins to become a problem to this Soldier when they receive nothing in return. You may have to question the sincerity of the deed, when they start looking for some type of praise or reward because they did what they are supposed to do as a leader.

The willing but unable Soldier is the one that will do everything in their power to meet the mission but needs that steady guidance to ensure they are going in the right direction. This type of Soldier is very loyal and dedicated but does not know how to make things happen. Either they are afraid to make mistakes or just not confident in their abilities because of past inaccuracies. You have to be careful with this Soldier because you do not want to lose this person by pushing too hard or not pushing hard enough. This Soldier is the one that needs a lot of nurturing with the intent of turning this person into a willing and able Soldier. You have to continue to challenge this person with increased responsibility, but the challenge cannot be so difficult that they will become so frustrated that their loyalty and dedication comes into question. The key to this person is the right balance of guidance and responsibility.

The unwilling but able Soldier, I also stated that the "Gray Zone Soldier" is the one that would rather spend all of their time trying to find ways to get out of work instead of doing what it takes to get the mission accomplished. They encompass the tools the willing and able Soldier has but for some reason is unwilling to do so. This Soldier can be cancerous in your organization because they are always trying to undermine the leadership. Everything around them is more important than mission accomplishment. They tend to let outside influences or past behaviors guide them down the wrong roads. They'd rather blame others for their lack of success rather than taking full advantage of their own skills to achieve more in their careers. Most of the time, they are the biggest underachievers in the organization and try to influence others to follow in their footsteps. Supervision for this type of Soldier is constant and will take a lot of your time. They will always just do enough not to get in trouble but, on the other hand, not enough to complete the mission. I will talk more about this type of Soldier later in the book.

The last type of Soldier is the unwilling and unable. They are just marking time in your organization until their era as a Soldier has come to an end. This Soldier requires 100 percent supervision because this Soldier, you will be spending 90 percent of your time with that 10 percent Soldier. With this type of Soldier, you just have to make sure that your paperwork is in order so when it is time to process this Soldier for separation, there will not be any obstruction.

2. Leader Actions are legal, ethical, and moral. This is part of an NCOs decision-making process. Get it right or pay the consequences.

As a leader, you have to know right from wrong. This is a simple statement but has the most power. I will always say that as long as you are doing the right thing, then you shouldn't have anything to worry about getting in a difficult state of affairs. People start to get in trouble when they know the right thing to do but make that conscious decision by doing the wrong thing instead. You have to take your personal feelings out of your decision-making and interject the legal, ethical, and moral thing into it. This is where a leader's creditability comes into question when you allow your personal feelings to come into play. If you keep it legal, ethical, and moral to the best of your knowledge and not your ability, then you will not have to worry about doing the right thing. The reason I said to the best of your knowledge is because, as a leader it is your job to stay up on what is legal, ethical, and morally right. You have too many channels or outlets to find out the right answers to situations instead of making up your own. When you begin to make up your own rules, you will always have to worry about the decision you make coming back at you where you have to pay consequences in the end. One of the consequences you will have to pay is your reputation as a leader of having poor legal, ethical, and moral standards, and negativity of that magnitude will be very difficult to overcome. Another major consequence is the fact that you might get relieved of your position or legal action against you.

3. It is lonely at the top. Accept it or fail. The best leaders are OK with standing alone if their moral principles are right.

A true leader has the confidence to stand alone. No matter how you try to find a rationale for it, as a leader, you are not going to satisfy everyone with the decisions you make. I have always said that when you make a decision, a third of the people are going to like it, a third is going to hate it, and the last third it just doesn't matter either way. So, once you learn and understand that you are not going to make everyone happy, then you just realize that you need to make decisions that are best for everyone involved. See, you don't make the decision based on popularity but what is right. This is not going to gain you many friends, but you can sleep at night knowing you didn't sacrifice your morals for a few more invitations to a party or BBQ.

4. Be FAIR, Be FAIR, and Be FAIR. NCOs will enforce fairness more than they will discipline or anything else. Educate and mentor those around you, junior officers especially.

This is easy to say, unfortunately harder to do because what may be fair to you might not be fair to everyone else. That is why you will enforce fairness more than anything else. Your subordinates will follow you to the end of the world as long as they perceive you as a fair person. Most people do not desire more than anyone else, but they don't want less either, especially when it comes to fairness. People are much happier with their leadership if they think everyone is getting treated fairly, no one is getting more than anyone else. If your subordinates can see the leadership treating the so-called favorite just like everyone else, then you are less likely to have complaints about your leadership style. If anything has to be a constant in your leadership, it is the fact that you are fair, and you treat everyone with fairness no matter the situation and your personal feelings or beliefs about that person.

5. You knew it was a snake when you picked it up, so don't get upset when the snake bites you.

The story goes like this, there was this old retiree walking home and saw this snake on the side of the road, mangled and sick. The retiree being the old Soldier decided to pick the snake up and take it home. Once the retiree got the snake inside, the retiree bandaged and gave the snake medicine to help the snake get well again. After a few days, the snake was well enough to leave. The retiree was standing by the fire as the snake was about to go outside; the snake stopped and turned to look at the retiree and began to slide back towards the retiree. The retiree thought the snake came back to thank them for taking care of him, but the snake bit the retiree in the leg. The retiree fell to the floor as the snake began to leave again. The retiree called to the snake before he went outside and asked him why he bit him after he brought him into his house, fed him, and nursed him back to health. The snake turned around and told the retiree, "You knew what I was when you picked me up." I really enjoy this parable because it holds true for so many people trying to save someone who cannot or don't want to be saved. A lot of leaders get into this situation because they try to change a snake's behavior. The leader knows that this person is up to no good but still puts their reputation on the line by recommending this person for a promotion or an award then this person turns right around and bites them because they continue with their same pattern of bad behavior. One example, when I was a 1SG (First Sergeant), I had this NCO working for me as my training NCO. This NCO worked for me for about eight months, and I never recommended him for promotion because he just didn't possess the skills and dedication needed for the next pay grade. I moved him to another clinic and in less than a month time, the NCOIC (Noncommissioned Officer in Charge) recommended him for the promotion board. I asked the NCOIC, what did this NCO show you in a month that he could not show me in eight months that would make you deem it necessary by recommending him for promotion. He did not have one, so I told him to deal with the outcome. After the NCO received what he wanted and that was his promotable status, he started to give the NCOIC problems. The NCOIC called me and asked me to move him, and I told him to deal with the snake bite.

6. If you are in charge of a room full of Soldiers and they are not getting along, you simply put them ALL on the same sheet of music. Make sure you let them know who is in charge and what direction you are headed.

I always ask my NCOs this scenario for a way for me to find out their thought process when it comes to taking charge as a leader. You are brand-new to the unit, and you are put in charge of ten Soldiers. Your supervisor tells you the ten Soldiers don't get along. They are all different races, religions, ethnic backgrounds, and anything else you can think of that causes people not to get along. At your first meeting with the ten Soldiers, what do you do or say to them? I have heard everything from taking them to lunch, to a team-building exercise, or sitting down and talking to all of them individually. There are no wrong answers because it is based on your leadership style, but what you have to realize is that time is always a factor. You have a mission, and you need your team to work as a unit. They have to work like your fingers and thumb on your hand. That is your job as a leader to get whomever you are in charge of to work together as one single entity. One of my favorite movies is *Remember the Titans*. One of the scenes I loved and started to use when I was a drill sergeant was when the head coach had the football players in spring training. The black and white players were not getting along. The first thing he did was to let them know who was in charge. Secondly, he made the offense and defense eat together and share a room. Then he made them learn about a teammate of a different race, and if they didn't, the practices became harder.

Eventually, they started getting along and working together because they found out that even though they were different races, they had the same interest, which was football. As a leader, you have to figure it out, get your workforces working together or the mission will suffer. Number six, seven, eight, and nine in my philosophy go hand in hand.

7. Enter a new unit "kicking the door down" no matter your rank. Show your seniors, peers, and subordinates that you are disciplined, trustworthy, by the book, and won't take any crap.

8. A disciplined Soldier is a happy Soldier. They don't always know that, but it's not our job to convince them of this. They will thank you and appreciate it later.

9. Discipline and accountability come before improving morale. Enforce these two things and morale will automatically improve. It is impossible to try and improve morale if discipline is lacking.

10. Contrary to popular belief, Leadership isn't Liker-ship. A leader who befriends their Soldiers has done so because they couldn't find anybody else to be friends with. It will always lead to problems. Is that Soldier paying your bills or going to get you promoted? If none of the above applies to you, then you need to stop trying to be their buddy. If one of them applies, then you have bigger problems. This is a quick way to lose your power base with your Soldiers.

Leadership is not liker-ship! You will have to choose one or the other. If you want the leadership track, then being liked is not for you. If you want the liker-ship track, then being an effective leader is not for you. The two don't get along. Don't get it confused with being a likable person. You can be a likable person and still choose leadership over liker-ship. Where the confusion comes in is when you let liker-ship make decisions for you. If you are trying to be liked based on the decisions you make, then you are using liker-ship. If you are making a decision based on your moral principles and just happen to be a likable person, then you are using leadership. You really don't go into a leadership position for accolades or friendships but to make a positive difference in one's unit and hopefully your subordinate's lives. It should be the hardest and most rewarding job in a person's career. Every decision you make will affect someone under your command, and that task should never be taken lightly. Once you start making a decision based on friendships or to obtain friendships, your judgment will always lead to problems. You have to make a decision based on the welfare of the majority and not the benefit of the minority.

11. You can't turn chicken_ _ _ _ into chicken salad. No matter what you add to it (rank or otherwise) it will still be that same chicken_ _ _ _.

Various people think, if you give someone a promotion or a new position, then that will change them. Regardless of how many stars, bars, or stripes you put on certain people, they will still be that same appalling leader they were at the previous rank or position they had before. The only way you can prevent this is to stop them earlier in their careers. This is a classic case of not wanting to "hurt" someone's career. You know when someone is not a person that needs to lead people. Leaders do this a lot to make their stats look good by having more promotions than discipline issues. Leaders fail to counsel that substandard individual to tell them what they need to do to improve their performance, so they end up letting those people advance instead of keeping them at their current grade. Then the supervisor hopes by letting them get promoted, they will miraculously improve their subpar behavior. If they are getting promoted the way they are, then why should they change until someone steps up and requires them to change for the better or get left behind. We need to stop the mess-up-and-move-up mentality.

12. Teaching is mostly about listening, and learning is mostly about talking. When the student is ready to learn, then the teacher is ready to teach.

This is the reason we have two ears and one mouth. You should listen twice as much as you should speak.

13. Counseling is about the past, Coaching/Teaching is about the present, and Mentoring is about the future.

When you counsel, you are educating your subordinates what they did right, wrong, and what they should have done better for that particular situation or event. Coaching and teaching are about instructing someone through a current problem or state of affairs. Mentoring is in relation to having a discussion with your subordinates on your expectations of them and their potential as a leader.

14. Your attitude shapes your aptitude, which in turn, controls your altitude.

Your outlook on a situation forms your capacity to learn, which will manage how high you are able to move ahead. People like to deal with positive people. Leaders will deal with you further if you stay positive and have a wiliness to learn.

15. A true leader has the confidence to stand alone, the courage to make tough decisions, and compassion to listen to the needs of others. He does not set out to be a leader, but becomes one by the quality of his actions and the integrity of his intent. In the end, leaders are much like eagles... they don't flock; you find them one at a time.

16. Never make someone a priority when you are only an option for them.

This has a lot to do with mentorship, to me, more than anything else. You try to push someone when they are not ready to be pushed, then they might fall instead of moving forward in the right direction. Therefore, if they are not ready to make their career the priority, then no matter how much you try to set time aside and talk to that person, then you are really wasting your time. You will be more like "break in case of emergency" instead of "use until complete." Once someone starts to get serious about what they want to do in their career or life, then you cannot get rid of them because you will see a positive change in their behavior. For example, sergeants major would set time aside for Soldiers to come and see them so they could review their records for the senior enlisted promotion boards. Some took them up on the offer, but most didn't. Consequently, for whatever reasons, those who didn't take the sergeants major up on their offer weren't really serious about their careers at the time. When you are trying to get promoted, you want everybody you can to have a look at your records because the more eyes the better, to see errors or mistakes you might have that the previous person may have missed. Furthermore, to me, that says that if I get promoted is okay, and if I don't, then that is okay too. In any type of relationship, both participants' roles are defined, and they share equally how the partnership will move forward. One cannot be the contributor while the observer gets involved when it is suitable for them. It will not work no matter how much you may want it to or how well your intentions may be for that person.

17. Never look back unless you plan on going that way – Henry David Thoreau. People evolve as their lives change, so you already know what was behind you, so there is no need to look that way. Always shoot for the moon because if you miss, then you will always be amongst the stars.

No unit, as a whole, is so good that it cannot be improved. You may have leadership ability and strengths of an excellent squad, platoon, section, or Junior/Senior NCO, but unless you take immediate steps to make it even better, it will begin to deteriorate. From the first day you stepped into a military uniform until the day you decide to hang it up permanently, you must strive to better yourself, your Soldiers, your Unit, and the Army. There is no rest, no relaxing, no slowing down, and no stopping. The Noncommissioned Officer is the "backbone of the Army." One of our objectives is to **KEEP THAT A REALITY!!!** This is my philosophy with the belief that it is from someone who is trying to help you, not criticize you. An honest, sincere self-evaluation at frequent intervals in your career is an excellent tool to keep you on your toes and assure yourself that you are a valuable asset.

There Isn't a Blueprint for Success

The institution, what I call the Army, is a great organization. The concept is amazing because the only way the leaders succeed is off the success of your subordinates. This is what makes this Fortune 500 company different from all of the rest. I have nothing against the rest of the organizations, but I have heard that most of the leaders try to retain a little information from their employer for job security. A lot of the times it is only one person in a section that knows that particular job.

There are no cross-training programs because, in the corporate world, you do and only do what is in your job description and nothing else. The Army is different because everyone in the unit will know what is going on and everyone will know everyone else's job just in case the leadership is out, the mission will go on without much interruption.

You will hear the saying over and over again that our most valuable resource is the people, which is true because you are going to leave the Army one way or another. No matter how you leave, you want to leave the organization in a better state of affairs than the way you found it.

The way you do that is making sure that, as a leader, you take a vested interest in the future leaders that are coming behind you. You cannot think the Army will survive if you keep all the information you have to yourself and not share it with your subordinates. The Army tells you what you need to do in order to move through the ranks and have a successful career.

The Army has a career map for each and every job skill in the inventory. You don't have to work that hard to find it because it is required, for your seniors, to have a copy for you during your quarterly counseling. Nevertheless, you cannot just come to work on time and don't cause trouble, then think you are able to stay in the Army for at least twenty years and retire. What makes the Army bad is a small group of people that get stuck in the gray zone.

The Gray Zone Leaders are the ones that allow complacency to penetrate their thought process and then display a bad example for the future leaders in their footprint of the Army to follow. There are many reasons leaders get stuck in the gray zone from not having a plan to get ahead at the beginning of their careers to blaming everyone else for their lack of motivation towards the end of their careers.

Whatever it is, leaders need to identify the Gray Zone Leaders and either change their mindsets to become a willing and able Soldier or remove them from the ranks before they can spread bad leadership throughout their area of influence. Not only will they influence their area but other areas also because if one of their subordinates goes to a new location, that same Gray Zone Leadership influence goes along with them.

Many times you cannot tell you have a Gray Zone Leader in your ranks especially if they are just arriving at your unit. They can hide their true behavior for a while, but eventually, it will begin to show. They will want you to think that they are willing and able as soon as they enter the unit. Certain circumstances will force them to take care of their subordinates. They will fail at that task or show the need to be micromanaged, and then you will see the unwillingness in their performance. Those are the ones that are right in front of your eyes, but the ones who have been in so long that they can hide it better or the ones that will take care of their responsibilities as long as it is for their advantage to get ahead and not because it is the right thing to do.

Many leaders like to take these kinds of Soldiers under their wing hoping to change their habits like it is a project and show everyone what type of leader they are, which is a rescuer of bad Soldiers. That is fine as long as the leader knows that the person has to have a desire to change in the first place, and you cannot change everybody. You will spend all your time and effort on someone who already knows in their own mind that they are happy with themselves.

The leader has to know going into this situation already knowing how long they are going to stay with this little undertaking of theirs. If the Gray Zone Leader has been what they think is successful in their mind, they have no intentions of changing their behavior.

Hence, if they don't come to you, then there is really no need to venture down that road only to find disappointment at the end of the line. Maybe they are looking for someone they can connect to who is not in the gray zone, but those are uncommon.

I am not saying it is not going to work, but what advantage would they have by doing it your way if their way has been working for them in the past. Always do what you can for any Soldier, but you have to know when enough is enough, to save yourself some time, and the Army's money, because every time a Gray Zone Leader goes to an ATM, they should wear a ski mask because they are robbing the government.

References

Frye, M. (1983). The Systemic Birdcage of Sexism. *The Politics of Reality*, 2-7.

Lewis, G. C. (2011). *Godly Mentorship*. Retrieved from www.angelcasiano.com: https://angelcasiano.com/2011/03/22/godly-mentorship-by-prophet-g-craige-lewis/

Merriam-Webster. (1828). *Merriam-Webster Dictionary*. Encyclopædia Britannica Company.

Moynihan, D. P. (n.d.). You're entitled to your own opinion. Retrieved from https://www.goodreads/quotes/

Oluyi, I. (2011). *How to Avoid Mistakes in Life by Learning from the Stories of Others*. Retrieved from TalkAfrique: http://www.talkafrique.com/career-tools/motivation-self-help/african-stories-mor

Powell, C. (n.d.). *The less you associate with some*. Retrieved from https://www.goodreads/quotes/310930-the-less-youassocite-with some-people-

Thoreau, H. D. (n.d.). *Good Reads*. Retrieved from www.goodreads.com: http://www.goodreads.com/quotes/62257-never-look-back-unless-you-are-planning-to-go-that

Unknown. (n.d.). *Xenogears*. Retrieved from Wikiquote: https://en.wikiquote.org/wiki/Xenogears

Williamson, M. (1992). Our Deepest Fear. In M. Williamson, *A Return to Love: Reflections on the Principles of "a Course in Miracles"* (pp. 190-191). Harper Collins.

Woodson, C. G. (1933). *The Mis-Education of the Negro*. Communication Systems.